MASTER T

The
Civil War
and
Reconstruction

About Peterson's

Peterson's® has been your trusted educational publisher for over 50 years. It's a milestone we're quite proud of, as we continue to offer the most accurate, dependable, high-quality educational content in the field, providing you with everything you need to succeed. No matter where you are on your academic or professional path, you can rely on Peterson's for its books, online information, expert test-prep tools, the most up-to-date education exploration data, and the highest quality career success resources—everything you need to achieve your education goals. For our complete line of products, visit www.petersons.com.

For more information, contact Peterson's, 8740 Lucent Blvd., Suite 400, Highlands Ranch, CO 80129; 800-338-3282 Ext. 54229; or find us online at **www.petersons.com**.

ISBN: 978-0-7689-4441-9

Printed in the United States of America

10 9 8 7 6 5 4 3 2 1   22 21 20

Contents

Before You Begin

HOW THIS BOOK IS ORGANIZED

Peterson's *Master the*™ *DSST*® *The Civil War and Reconstruction Exam* provides a diagnostic test, subject-matter review, and a post-test.

- **Diagnostic Test**—Twenty multiple-choice questions, followed by an answer key with detailed answer explanations
- **Assessment Grid**—A chart designed to help you identify areas that you need to focus on based on your test results
- **Subject-Matter Review**—General overview of the exam subject, followed by a review of the relevant topics and terminology covered on the exam
- **Post-test**—Sixty multiple-choice questions, followed by an answer key and detailed answer explanations

The purpose of the diagnostic test is to help you figure out what you know—or don't know. The twenty multiple-choice questions are similar to the ones found on the DSST exam, and they should provide you with a good idea of what to expect. Once you take the diagnostic test, check your answers to see how you did. Included with each correct answer is a brief explanation regarding why a specific answer is correct, and in many cases, why other options are incorrect. Use the assessment grid to identify the questions you miss so that you can spend more time reviewing that information later. As with any exam, knowing your weak spots greatly improves your chances of success.

Following the diagnostic test is a subject-matter review. The review summarizes the various topics covered on the DSST exam. Key terms are defined; important concepts are explained; and when appropriate, examples are provided. As you read the review, some of the information may seem familiar while other information may seem foreign. Again, take note of the unfamiliar because that will most likely cause you problems on the actual exam.

After studying the subject-matter review, you should be ready for the post-test. The post-test contains sixty multiple-choice items, and it will serve as a dry run for the real DSST exam. There are complete answer explanations at the end of the test.

OTHER DSST® PRODUCTS BY PETERSON'S

Books, flashcards, practice tests, and videos available online at **www.petersons.com/testprep/dsst**

- Art of the Western World
- Astronomy
- Business Mathematics
- Business Ethics in Society
- Civil War and Reconstruction
- Computing and Information Technology
- Criminal Justice
- Environmental Science
- Ethics In America
- Ethics in Technology
- Foundations of Education
- Fundamentals of Cybersecurity
- Fundamentals of College Algebra
- Fundamentals of Counseling
- General Anthropology
- Health and Human Development
- History of the Soviet Union
- History of the Vietnam War
- Human Resource Management
- Introduction to Business
- Introduction to Geography
- Introduction to Law Enforcement
- Introduction to World Religions
- Lifespan Developmental Psychology
- Math for Liberal Arts
- Management Information Systems
- Money and Banking
- Organizational Behavior
- Personal Finance
- Introduction to Geology
- Principles of Advanced English Composition
- Principles of Finance
- Principles of Public Speaking
- Principles of Statistics
- Principles of Supervision
- Substance Abuse
- Technical Writing

Like what you see? Get unlimited access to Peterson's full catalog of DSST practice tests, instructional videos, flashcards and more for **75% off the first month!** Go to **www.petersons.com/testprep/dsst** and use coupon code **DSST2020** at checkout. Offer expires July 1, 2021.

Chapter 1

All About the DSST® Exam

WHAT IS DSST®?

Previously known as the DANTES Subject Standardized Tests, the DSST program provides the opportunity for individuals to earn college credit for what they have learned outside of the traditional classroom. Accepted or administered at more than 1,900 colleges and universities nationwide and approved by the American Council on Education (ACE), the DSST program enables individuals to use the knowledge they have acquired outside the classroom to accomplish their educational and professional goals.

WHY TAKE A DSST® EXAM?

DSST exams offer a way for you to save both time and money in your quest for a college education. Why enroll in a college course in a subject you already understand? For more than 30 years, the DSST program has offered the perfect solution for individuals who are knowledgeable in a specific subject and want to save both time and money. A passing score on a DSST exam provides physical evidence to universities of proficiency in a specific subject. More than 1,900 accredited and respected colleges and universities across the nation award undergraduate credit for passing scores on DSST exams. With the DSST program, individuals can shave months off the time it takes to earn a degree.

The DSST program offers numerous advantages for individuals in all stages of their educational development:

- Adult learners
- College students
- Military personnel

Adult learners desiring college degrees face unique circumstances—demanding work schedules, family responsibilities, and tight budgets. Yet adult learners also have years of valuable work experience that can be applied toward a degree through the DSST program. For example, adult learners with on-the-job experience in business and management might be able to skip the Business 101 courses if they earn passing marks on DSST exams such as Introduction to Business and Principles of Supervision.

Adult learners can put their prior learning into action and move forward with more advanced course work. Adults who have never enrolled in a college course may feel a little uncertain about their abilities. If this describes your situation, then sign up for a DSST exam and see how you do. A passing score may be the boost you need to realize your dream of earning a degree. With family and work commitments, adult learners often feel they lack the time to attend college. The DSST program enables adult learners the unique opportunity to work toward college degrees without the time constraints of semester-long course work. DSST exams take two hours or less to complete. In one weekend, you could earn credit for multiple college courses.

The DSST exams also benefit students who are already enrolled in a college or university. With college tuition costs on the rise, most students face financial challenges. The fee for each DSST exam starts at $80 (plus administration fees charged by some testing facilities)—significantly less than the $750 average cost of a 3-hour college class. Maximize tuition assistance by taking DSST exams for introductory or mandatory course work. Once you earn a passing score on a DSST exam, you are free to move on to higher-level course work in that subject matter, take desired electives, or focus on courses in a chosen major.

Not only do college students and adult learners profit from DSST exams, but military personnel reap the benefits as well. If you are a member of the armed services at home or abroad, you can initiate your post-military career by taking DSST exams in areas with which you have experience. Military personnel can gain credit anywhere in the world, thanks to the fact that almost all of the tests are available through the internet at designated testing locations. DSST testing facilities are located at more than 500 military installations, so service members on active duty can get a jump-start on a post-military career with the DSST program. As an additional incentive, DANTES (Defense Activity for Non-Traditional Education Support) provides funding for DSST test fees for eligible members of the military.

More than 30 subject-matter tests are available in the fields of Business, Humanities, Math, Physical Science, Social Sciences, and Technology.

Available DSST® Exams

Business	Social Sciences
Business Ethics and Society	A History of the Vietnam War
Business Mathematics	Art of the Western World
Computing and Information Technology	Criminal Justice
Human Resource Management	Foundations of Education
Introduction to Business	Fundamentals of Counseling
Management Information Systems	General Anthropology
Money and Banking	History of the Soviet Union
Organizational Behavior	Introduction to Geography
Personal Finance	Introduction to Law Enforcement
Principles of Finance	Lifespan Developmental Psychology
Principles of Supervision	Substance Abuse
	The Civil War and Reconstruction

Humanities	Physical Sciences
Ethics in America	Astronomy
Introduction to World Religions	Environmental Science
Principles of Advanced English	Health and Human Development
Composition	Introduction to Geology
Principles of Public Speaking	

Math	Technology
Fundamentals of College Algebra	Ethics in Technology
Math for Liberal Arts	Fundamentals of Cybersecurity
Principles of Statistics	Technical Writing

As you can see from the table, the DSST program covers a wide variety of subjects. However, it is important to ask two questions before registering for a DSST exam.

1. Which universities or colleges award credit for passing DSST exams?
2. Which DSST exams are the most relevant to my desired degree and my experience?

Knowing which universities offer DSST credit is important. In all likelihood, a college in your area awards credit for DSST exams, but find out before taking an exam by contacting the university directly. Then review the list of DSST exams to determine which ones are most relevant to the degree you are seeking and to your base of knowledge. Schedule an appointment with your college adviser to determine which exams best fit your degree program and which college courses the DSST exams can replace. Advisers should also be able to tell you the minimum score required on the DSST exam to receive university credit.

DSST® TEST CENTERS

You can find DSST testing locations in community colleges and universities across the country. Check the DSST website (**www.getcollegecredit. com**) for a location near you or contact your local college or university to find out if the school administers DSST exams. Keep in mind that some universities and colleges administer DSST exams only to enrolled students. DSST testing is available to men and women in the armed services at more than 500 military installations around the world.

HOW TO REGISTER FOR A DSST® EXAM

Once you have located a nearby DSST testing facility, you need to contact the testing center to find out the exam administration schedule. Many centers are set up to administer tests via the internet, while others use printed materials. Almost all DSST exams are available as online tests, but the method used depends on the testing center. The cost for each DSST exam starts at $80, and many testing locations charge a fee to cover their costs for administering the tests. Credit cards are the only accepted payment method for taking online DSST exams. Credit card, certified check, and money order are acceptable payment methods for paper-and-pencil tests.

Test takers are allotted two score reports—one mailed to them and another mailed to a designated college or university, if requested. Online tests generate unofficial scores at the end of the test session, while individuals taking paper tests must wait four to six weeks for score reports.

PREPARING FOR A DSST® EXAM

Even though you are knowledgeable in a certain subject matter, you should still prepare for the test to ensure you achieve the highest score possible. The first step in studying for a DSST exam is to find out what will be on the specific test you have chosen. Information regarding test content is located on the DSST fact sheets, which can be downloaded at no cost from **www. getcollegecredit.com**. Each fact sheet outlines the topics covered on a subject-matter test, as well as the approximate percentage assigned to each topic. For example, questions on the Civil War and Reconstruction exam are distributed in the following way: Causes of the War–16%, 1861–11%, 1862–17%, 1863–19%, 1864–15%, 1865–7%, and Reconstruction–15%.

In addition to the breakdown of topics on a DSST exam, the fact sheet also lists recommended reference materials. If you do not own the recommended books, then check college bookstores. Avoid paying high prices for new textbooks by looking online for used textbooks. Don't panic if you are unable to locate a specific textbook listed on the fact sheet; the textbooks are merely recommendations. Instead, search for comparable books used in university courses on the specific subject. Current editions are ideal, and it is a good idea to use at least two references when studying for a DSST exam. Of course, the subject matter provided in this book will be a sufficient review for most test takers. However, if you need additional information, then it is a good idea to have some of the reference materials at your disposal when preparing for a DSST exam.

Fact sheets include other useful information in addition to a list of reference materials and topics. Each fact sheet includes subject-specific sample questions like those you will encounter on the DSST exam. The sample questions provide an idea of the types of questions you can expect on the exam. Test questions are multiple-choice with one correct answer and three incorrect choices.

The fact sheet also includes information about the number of credit hours that ACE has recommended be awarded by colleges for a passing DSST exam score. However, you should keep in mind that not all universities and colleges adhere to the ACE recommendation for DSST credit hours. Some institutions require DSST exam scores higher than the minimum score recommended by ACE. Once you have acquired appropriate reference materials and you have the outline provided on the fact sheet, you are ready to start studying, which is where this book can help.

TEST DAY

After reviewing the material and taking practice tests, you are finally ready to take your DSST exam. Follow these tips for a successful test day experience.

1. **Arrive on time.** Not only is it courteous to arrive on time to the DSST testing facility, but it also allows plenty of time for you to take care of check-in procedures and settle into your surroundings.
2. **Bring identification.** DSST test facilities require that candidates bring a valid government-issued identification card with a current photo and signature. Acceptable forms of identification include a current driver's license, passport, military identification card, or state-issued identification card. Individuals who fail to bring proper identification to the DSST testing facility will not be allowed to take an exam.
3. **Bring the right supplies.** If your exam requires the use of a calculator, you may bring a calculator that meets the specifications. For paper-based exams, you may also bring No. 2 pencils with an eraser and black ballpoint pens. Regardless of the exam methodology, you are NOT allowed to bring reference or study materials, scratch paper, or electronics such as cell phones, personal handheld devices, cameras, alarm wrist watches, or tape recorders to the testing center.
4. **Take the test.** During the exam, take the time to read each question-and-answer option carefully. Eliminate the choices you know are incorrect to narrow the number of potential answers. If a question completely stumps you, take an educated guess and move on—remember that DSSTs are timed; you will have 2 hours to take the exam.

With the proper preparation, DSST exams will save you both time and money. So join the thousands of people who have already reaped the benefits of DSST exams and move closer than ever to your college degree.

THE CIVIL WAR AND RECONSTRUCTION EXAM FACTS

The DSST® The Civil War and Reconstruction exam consists of 100 multiple-choice questions that cover material commonly found in a college-level course, including pre-secession and causes of the war, secession, Fort Sumter, major battles, the political climate, the assassination of Abraham Lincoln, the end of the Confederacy, and Reconstruction.

Area or Course Equivalent: The Civil War and Reconstruction
Level: Lower-level baccalaureate
Amount of Credit: 3 Semester Hours
Minimum Score: 400
Source: https://www.getcollegecredit.com/wp-content/assets/fact-sheets/TheCivilWarAndReconstruction.pdf

I. **Causes of the War – 16%**

    a. United States Society in the Mid-Nineteenth Century

    b. Slavery

    c. Anti-Slavery and Abolition movement

    d. Westward Expansion of Free and Slave Territory

    e. John Brown's raid on Harper's Ferry

    f. Political situation in 1860

II. **1861 – 11%**

    a. Secession

    b. Formation of Confederacy

    c. Fort Sumter

    d. Lincoln's Call for Volunteers

    e. First Manassas (Bull Run)

    f. Union Army versus Confederate Army

    g. Lincoln versus Davis leadership

III. **1862 – 17%**

    a. Southern Strategy

    b. War in the East

    c. War in the West

    d. Major Battles

    e. Emancipation Proclamation

IV. **1863 – 19%**

    a. Casualties

    b. Role of Women in the War

    c. Black Americans and the War

    d. Major Battles

V. 1864 – 15%

    a. Political Situation

    b. War in the West

    c. War in the East

VI. 1865 – 7%

    a. Sherman's Carolina Campaign

    b. Fall of Richmond

    c. Lee's Surrender

    d. Assassination of Lincoln

    e. End of the Confederacy

    f. Cost of the War

VII. Reconstruction – 15%

    a. Presidential Reconstruction Plans

    b. Southern Response

    c. Congressional Reconstruction Plans

    d. Military Reconstruction

    e. End of Reconstruction

Chapter 2

The Civil War and Reconstruction Diagnostic Test

DIAGNOSTIC TEST ANSWER SHEET

1. Ⓐ Ⓑ Ⓒ Ⓓ

2. Ⓐ Ⓑ Ⓒ Ⓓ

3. Ⓐ Ⓑ Ⓒ Ⓓ

4. Ⓐ Ⓑ Ⓒ Ⓓ

5. Ⓐ Ⓑ Ⓒ Ⓓ

6. Ⓐ Ⓑ Ⓒ Ⓓ

7. Ⓐ Ⓑ Ⓒ Ⓓ

8. Ⓐ Ⓑ Ⓒ Ⓓ

9. Ⓐ Ⓑ Ⓒ Ⓓ

10. Ⓐ Ⓑ Ⓒ Ⓓ

11. Ⓐ Ⓑ Ⓒ Ⓓ

12. Ⓐ Ⓑ Ⓒ Ⓓ

13. Ⓐ Ⓑ Ⓒ Ⓓ

14. Ⓐ Ⓑ Ⓒ Ⓓ

15. Ⓐ Ⓑ Ⓒ Ⓓ

16. Ⓐ Ⓑ Ⓒ Ⓓ

17. Ⓐ Ⓑ Ⓒ Ⓓ

18. Ⓐ Ⓑ Ⓒ Ⓓ

19. Ⓐ Ⓑ Ⓒ Ⓓ

20. Ⓐ Ⓑ Ⓒ Ⓓ

THE CIVIL WAR AND RECONSTRUCTION DIAGNOSTIC TEST

Directions: Carefully read each of the following 20 questions. Choose the best answer to each question and fill in the corresponding circle on the answer sheet. The Answer Key and Explanations can be found following this Diagnostic Test.

1. Popular sovereignty was established by which of the following?

   A. Missouri Compromise
   B. Kansas-Nebraska Act
   C. Dred Scott decision
   D. Republican Party

2. *The Liberator* was most notable for what reason?

   A. It was the most famous train on the Underground Railroad.
   B. It was the nickname for Abraham Lincoln, after he issued the Emancipation Proclamation.
   C. It was the first American ironclad.
   D. It was an anti-slavery publication founded by William Lloyd Garrison.

3. How did the plantation system hurt the voting strength of the South?

   A. Because the plantations were so spread out but took up so much land there was room for fewer people in the South.
   B. Slaves were still counted at three-fifths for voting, so smaller plantations did not have as many votes as large plantations.
   C. Plantation owners rarely voted because their political power in local government was done primarily through illegal means.
   D. Each plantation only counted as one vote regardless of the number of men on it.

4. Why was Lincoln's election a catalyst for southern secession?

   A. Lincoln had campaigned on a hard platform of banning slavery.
   B. Lincoln believed in breaking up large southern plantations.
   C. Lincoln had won the election without a single southern vote.
   D. Lincoln promised to go to war with the South if elected.

5. What major advantage did the Confederacy have at the start of the Civil War?

   A. The Confederacy had a larger population.
   B. The Confederacy had European aid.
   C. The Confederacy was fighting a defensive war.
   D. The Confederacy held a majority of the country's railroads.

6. Which battle allowed President Lincoln to issue the Emancipation Proclamation?

   A. Second Battle of Bull Run
   B. Antietam
   C. Gettysburg
   D. Appomattox

7. The Emancipation Proclamation proclaimed slaves to be

   A. free in all Union states.
   B. free in all border states.
   C. free in all Confederate states.
   D. free in all states.

8. Which general took control of the Union in their campaign for the West in 1862?

   A. George B. McClellan
   B. Ambrose Burnside
   C. Ulysses S. Grant
   D. William T. Sherman

9. How did the battle of the *Monitor* versus *Merrimac* mark a turning point?

    A. It was the end of wooden ships with naval warfare being replaced by ironclads.

    B. The Confederate victory brought European aid to their cause.

    C. The Union victory allowed President Lincoln to be reelected.

    D. The Union defeat led to a call to institute the draft.

10. New opportunities arose for women during the Civil War including the ability to take part in which field?

    A. Military officers

    B. Nurses

    C. Plantation owners

    D. Government office employees

11. How did African American soldiers face prejudice during the war?

    A. Former slaves were forced to take a loyalty oath to the Union before serving.

    B. Escaped slaves were not allowed to fight for the Union.

    C. African American generals were given the lowest number of troops to command.

    D. African Americans were segregated into all black units.

12. The Battle of Gettysburg's effect on the war was which of the following?

    A. The Confederate victory prolonged the war and forced the Union to institute the draft.

    B. The Confederate loss left Lee to retreat and the South never regained the offensive.

    C. The Union victory led to the Emancipation Proclamation.

    D. The Union loss forced Lincoln to publicly shame his generals and replace them.

13. How did Massachusetts' 54th Regiment change the course of the Civil War in 1863?

    A. Their victory in the western campaign pushed Confederate forces away from the Mississippi River.

    B. Their surprise invasion of southern Pennsylvania on Union forces led to the greatest causalities of the war.

    C. The regiment was the first all-black union in the war.

    D. The regiment was the first to employ a black general with white soldiers.

14. Who ran against Abraham Lincoln in the election of 1864?

    A. Former General George McClellan

    B. Former slave Frederick Douglass

    C. Confederate President Jefferson Davis

    D. War Democrat Andrew Johnson

15. Sherman's victory in Atlanta was significant for what reason?

    A. Confederate hopes for European aid ended.

    B. Confederate morale and volunteers increased dramatically.

    C. It secured the Mississippi River and New Orleans port for the Union.

    D. It secured Lincoln's reelection in 1864.

16. General Grant's western campaigns in 1864 were successful due to his strategy of

    A. attrition.

    B. using black soldiers.

    C. guerilla warfare.

    D. blockades.

17. What Union victory at the end of the Civil War was important because it destroyed the symbolic center of the Confederacy?

    A. Vicksburg

    B. Richmond

    C. Gettysburg

    D. Appomattox

18. How would Lincoln's Reconstruction plan be described as compared to Congress' plan?

A. Lincoln's was harsher to the Confederacy than that of Congress.

B. Lincoln's was similar to that of Congress.

C. Lincoln's was more lenient than that of Congress.

D. Lincoln did not have a plan as he was assassinated.

19. Congressional Reconstruction was dominated by which political party?

A. Republicans

B. Democrats

C. Whigs

D. Southern plantation owners

20. Reconstruction in the South was characterized by which of the following?

A. Failure to transition to a new, industrialized, and socially equitable society

B. Continued economic success and a new, diversified labor force

C. Favorable decisions made between former Confederate and Union leaders to increase the infrastructure of the South

D. Increased participation and economic success for former slaves

ANSWER KEY AND EXPLANATIONS

1. B	5. C	9. A	13. C	17. B
2. D	6. B	10. B	14. A	18. C
3. A	7. C	11. D	15. D	19. A
4. C	8. C	12. B	16. A	20. A

1. **The correct answer is B.** The Kansas-Nebraska Act divided the territories into two parts and allowed each to decide whether to allow slavery or not. This idea of allowing people to vote on expanding slavery or not is known as popular sovereignty. Choice A is incorrect because the Missouri Compromise created a specific line in which slavery could not expand. Choice C is incorrect because this case, while allowing slavery to spread, did not allow the people to vote on the decision. Choice D is incorrect because the Republican Party opposed the idea of popular sovereignty when proposed by Democrat Stephen A. Douglas.

2. **The correct answer is D.** *The Liberator* was an anti-slavery newspaper published by known abolitionist William Lloyd Garrison. The paper was in existence for almost 30 years and continually pushed for an immediate and absolute end to slavery. Choices A, B, and C are incorrect because *The Liberator* was a newspaper.

3. **The correct answer is A.** The size of plantations made it difficult for many to be in a given area, which lowered the population capabilities and number of voters in the south. There were more people living in the North because more could fit. Choice B is incorrect because counting slaves actually gave southerners more strength than without. However, the statement that large plantations were at an advantage is not relevant to the prompt. Choice C is incorrect because there is no evidence for this statement to be true; while many were involved in politics a good number did so legally and also voted often. Choice D is incorrect because it is false; votes were based on people not plantations.

4. **The correct answer is C.** Abraham Lincoln was not elected by a popular vote but carried all but one free state in the North, winning the electoral vote. No electoral vote from the South went to Lincoln yet he was able to become the 16th President. Choices A, B, and D are incorrect because they are all false statements. Lincoln ran on platforms that were the opposite of all the incorrect choices.

5. **The correct answer is C.** The Civil War was fought primarily on southern soil, with the Union needing to take the offensive and have a decisive win to end the battle. The Confederacy was able to fight a defensive war, on its own soil, that needed only to end in a draw for secession to hold. Choices A, B, and D are all incorrect as they are all false statements. The Confederacy had fewer people, no foreign aid (only a hope for one), and fewer railroads.

6. **The correct answer is B.** The draw encouraged Lincoln while keeping European aid from reaching the Confederate Army. Lincoln used the battle as a way to shift the focus of the war onto slavery. Choice A is incorrect because the Union took a loss at both battles of Bull Run. Choice C is incorrect because Gettysburg came after the proclamation was announced. Choice D is incorrect because it was not a battle.

7. **The correct answer is C.** The Proclamation declared all slaves in states of "rebellion" to be "then, thenceforward, and forever free." However, as Lincoln was not president of the Confederate states, the Proclamation freed little to no slaves. Choices A, B, and D are incorrect because the Proclamation did not declare slaves to be free in any of these places.

8. **The correct answer is C.** President Lincoln changed generals many times but finally found one that would continually defeat the Confederates in Ulysses Grant. Grant was in charge of gaining New Orleans and the Mississippi River in 1862 before being selected to control all the Union Army by 1864. Choices A, B, and D are incorrect because they were not generals in charge of the Western campaign. McClellan and Burnside were, at one point, each head of the Union Army (with Burnside replacing McClellan in 1862) and Sherman was placed under Grant's command.

9. **The correct answer is A.** This was the last time wooden ships were used in maritime battle. Ironclads would become the primary ships for naval battle moving forward as they were less vulnerable than wooden ships. Choice B is incorrect because European aid never came to the Confederacy. Choice C is incorrect because Lincoln was not reelected until 1864 and the battle was in 1862. Choice D is incorrect because a draft was not instituted after the battle.

10. **The correct answer is B.** Men had only been doctors and nurses prior to the Civil War. However, women stepped in to fill their roles, as they did in other sectors, when so many men were off fighting. Choice A is incorrect because women could not serve as military officers. Choice C is incorrect; although many women did take over farms and plantations because of the battles, becoming a plantation owner was not a new opportunity (just perhaps a more likely one than it had been before). Choice D is incorrect because women could not run for political office.

11. **The correct answer is D.** The 54th Massachusetts was an example of an all-black regiment that was created during the Civil War. African Americans could fight, but not with whites. This is a practice that would continue into the 1950s in American wars. Choice A is incorrect as there was no oath required. Choice B is incorrect because escaped slaves could and did fight for the Union. Choice C is incorrect because there were no African American generals.

12. **The correct answer is B.** The victory included more than 50,000 casualties over three days. After the unsuccessful charge by George Pickett left a crucial part of the Confederate Army destroyed, Lee was forced to retreat to Virginia. Choice A is incorrect because the Union was victorious. Choice C is incorrect because the Proclamation had been issued months prior after the Battle of Antietam. Choice D is incorrect because the Union was victorious.

13. **The correct answer is C.** The use of black troops, while segregated, marked a turning point in the war and American history. The 54th took a group of all black soldiers into battle under a white general and gained the nickname "Army of Freedom." Choice A is incorrect because the regiment did not fight in the battle for the Mississippi River in the west. Choice B is incorrect because the regiment did not fight for the Confederates. Choice D is incorrect because the regiment was all black with a white general (there were no black generals during the Civil War).

14. **The correct answer is A.** McClellan had been the head of the Union Army on more than one occasion and ran against Lincoln, on a platform of making peace with the Confederates. Choices B, C, and D are incorrect because they were not opponents of Lincoln in the election.

15. **The correct answer is D.** Sherman's victory in Atlanta and "March to the Sea" employed a total war tactic that destroyed the Confederate's remaining infrastructure and broke the spirit of its soldiers. Choice A is incorrect because European aid had long been avoided due to Union victories. Choice B is incorrect because Confederate morale was destroyed by the Union victory. Choice C is incorrect because both the Mississippi River and New Orleans had been secured years prior by General Grant.

16. **The correct answer is A.** Grant believed in wearing down his enemy and destroying their lines of supply until they surrendered. He continued to drag out battles for months and eventually reduced Lee's army. Choice B is incorrect because black soldiers alone were not enough to help win in the Western campaigns. Choice C is incorrect because Grant did not use this type of fighting. Choice D is incorrect because blockades were not possible in Western territories.

17. **The correct answer is B.** The victory at Richmond was symbolic because it served as the Confederate capital and heart of their country. The defeat marked the unofficial end to the war, as many saw no need to continue. Choices A, C, and D are incorrect because they were not symbolically relevant to the Confederate cause.

18. **The correct answer is C.** Lincoln proposed the ten percent plan, which allowed more Confederate states to re-enter the Union, and more quickly. Choice A is incorrect because Congress's plan was more harsh, requiring fifty percent to Lincoln's ten percent of Confederates having to pledge loyalty to the Union for reentry. Choice B is incorrect because the plans were different—Lincoln's plan was ten percent compared to Congress's fifty percent. Choice D is incorrect because Lincoln had begun to develop a plan as early as 1863.

19. **The correct answer is A.** Known as "Radical Republicans," the party of Lincoln had control of Congress and after Lincoln's death controlled the Reconstruction process. Choices B, C, and D are incorrect because they were not the controlling political parties.

20. **The correct answer is A.** Much of the South remained stuck in pre-Civil War times, with industrialization halted by a lack of (or damaged) infrastructure with Jim Crow laws and sharecropping that attempted to continue racism against African Americans. Choice B is incorrect because economic success from cotton production decreased as the labor forced remained similar to what it was before war with sharecropping. Choice C is incorrect because many decisions made were not favorable towards the South, with the planter aristocracy remaining in place and little attempt to industrialize happening. Choice D is incorrect because former slaves saw little economic success in the South in the years following the war.

DIAGNOSTIC TEST ASSESSMENT GRID

Now that you've completed the diagnostic test and read through the answer explanations, you can use your results to target your studying. Find the question numbers from the diagnostic test that you answered incorrectly and highlight or circle them below. Then focus extra attention on the sections dealing with those topics.

The Civil War and Reconstruction		
Content Area	**Topic**	**Question #**
Causes of the War	• United States society in the mid-nineteenth century • Slavery • Anti-slavery and abolition movement • Westward expansion of free and slave territory • John Brown's raid on Harper's Ferry • Political situation in 1860	1, 2, 3
1861	• Secession • Formation of confederacy • Fort Sumter • Lincoln's call for volunteers • First Manassas (Bull Run) • Union Army versus Confederate Army • Lincoln versus Davis leadership	4, 5
1862	• Southern strategy • War in the East • War in the West • Major battles • Emancipation Proclamation	6, 7, 8, 9
1863	• Casualties • Role of women in the war • Black Americans and the war • Major battles	10, 11, 12, 13

The Civil War and Reconstruction

1864	• Political situation • War in the West • War in the East	14, 15, 16
1865	• Sherman's Carolina Campaign • Fall of Richmond • Lee's surrender • Assassination of Lincoln • End of the Confederacy • Cost of the war	17
Reconstruction	• Presidential reconstruction plans • Southern response • Congressional reconstruction plans • Military reconstruction • End of reconstruction	18, 19, 20

Chapter 3

The Civil War and Reconstruction Subject Review

CAUSES OF THE WAR

United States in the Mid-Nineteenth Century

As the first half of the nineteenth century wore on, there were compromises made and politicians did their best to skate around major divisive issues, including the issue of slavery. By mid-century, the country had changed, and a greater focus was put on democracy, territorial expansion, and the future of the nation—these changes would lead to a divide that could not be quickly healed.

Industrialization

By the 1840s, the United States looked very different depending on where you lived. In the South, you could still find plantations and farmland reaching across the region but land was running out, and planting cotton was demanding on the soil. The North had begun transitioning into an industrial society, with factories replacing cottage industries and the transportation revolution evolving from canals to railroads.

The railroads connected the north to the west, and allowed for grains and foods to travel back and forth. This relationship helped grow the market economy of the United States, as well as created more interdependence between the regions.

Inside of northern factories, laborers were competing for jobs with new immigrants arriving from Europe. Tensions developed, as many of the lower-skilled positions were given to immigrants because they were willing to take less pay, leading to a nativist movement within the region (and the creation of such political parties as the Know-Nothings). Urbanization was taking over this part of the country, and the industrial growth led to a more diversified economy that would become a large strength for the Union during the Civil War.

The plantation system established in the South had little room for railroads or urban development; **King Cotton** had taken over both the South and the United States economy, and the region hungered for more land to grow cotton instead of a desire to industrialize. Because of the massive amount of land required for plantation life, the South had a smaller workforce but a larger role in the economy. By the start of the Civil War, the cotton industry would account for almost 57 percent of the United States' exports, so many in the region were eager for new farmable land. Most people living in the region were not plantation owners, however, and instead worked as small farmers or subsistence farmers. The South did benefit from the new technology created by industrialization, and sent much of its cotton to northern factories while also taking advantage of new advancements in farming tools.

TIP: King Cotton was the belief that economy and politically, cotton was king in southern society.

During the **antebellum period**, many reforms were taking place that changed the course of American society. One of the greatest reforms was known as the **Second Great Awakening**, a series of religious revivals that attempted to counter the rationalism and Puritan teachings of the previous decades. Much like the politics of the time, religion had become diverse and open to new groups and ideas. The movement itself saw many forms and groups, including the Baptists, Methodists, and Mormons, with a focus on the democratization of American society. Perhaps the greatest impact of the Second Great Awakening, however, was its influence on abolition and the war on slavery. With a renewed focus on religion, many in the North began to speak out against the sins of slavery and adopted a moral argument for ending the practice.

TIP: *Antebellum* period is a term used to describe the period before the Civil War.

The United States' population had more than doubled during the early half of the nineteenth century and it would double again leading into the 1850s. Birthrates were high during this period but immigration from European countries was also a key contributing factor. With the addition of new technology, manufacturing, transportation, and commercial agriculture the United States saw people living longer and enjoying more opportunities. Not only did wages increases, so too did the need for labor, leading to a higher standard of living and national economy.

The North continued to hold a population advantage due to compact living arrangements created by the new industrial centers. Factory life was more appealing to immigrants coming to America, as it did not require owning land, which helped to increase the number of people living in the northeast.

The South was fairly spread out, with almost 9 million of the nation's 23 million people living on small farms and larger plantations. Of those people, more than one-third were enslaved Africans who were forced into bondage as opposed to about 250,000 free African Americans found in the North (there were also about 250,000 free African Americans in the South).

Another key difference between the regions was their views on tariffs, as those in the North saw high tariffs as a way to protect American industries at the cost of southern profits. This issue would be raised time and again (most famously in the battle over the **Tariff of 1828**, otherwise known as the **Tariff of Abominations**), and had a large effect on creating the tension that would lead to the Civil War. Those in the south were at constant conflict with the raising of tariffs.

Slavery

Slavery had become synonymous with wealth in the south following the introduction of Eli Whitney's cotton gin in 1793. Although most people in the South did not actually own slaves, a degree of one's wealth and power was measured in land and slaves. Because there was a strict racial hierarchy in both the north and south, as well as an economic advantage to the practice, many people turned a blind eye to the practice for much of the early nineteenth century. However, as the North began to industrialize and manufacturing increased, many in the north no longer saw the economic necessity for slavery.

Also, with the aforementioned Second Great Awakening putting a greater emphasis on religion and democracy, **abolitionists** began to raise the question that had been previously ignored by the United States Constitution and politicians. Men like **John C. Calhoun** spoke out about slavery, referring to it as a "necessary evil." The North had been reaping the benefits of cotton production and the Union was economically strong because of it (a notion that southerners believed was validated by the **Panic of 1857**). There had historically been an unsaid agreement that slavery benefited both regions of the country for some time, and the South was prepared to defend its pro-slavery labor conditions.

> **TIP:** The United States Constitution did not mention the practice of slavery in America specifically; it did ban the use of the slave trade after 1808 and created the *Three-Fifths Compromise* for representation.

Anti-Slavery and Abolition Movement

Slave owners started to shift their defense of slavery away from being just economically beneficial to using religion, race, and standard of living as support for their "peculiar institution." Slave owners used scripture from the Bible to justify both slavery and racism against African Americans. They also looked to pseudo-science to falsely "prove" that Africans were better suited for slavery and even argued that conditions were better for slaves than those working in northern factories.

By mid-century, abolitionists began to speak out more, and two camps developed: **gradual abolitionists** and **immediate abolitionists**. Gradual abolitionists believed that slavery should be ended over time and allowed to die its own death, whereas immediate abolitionists wanted an abrupt end to slavery.

Abolitionists saw slavery as a sin and many, such as **William Lloyd Garrison**, took to new mediums to speak out against it. Garrison, a white abolitionist, began publishing an anti-slavery newspaper entitled *The Liberator*. The paper called for the immediate, and sometimes radical, abolition of slavery and would remain in publication for over 30 years.

Another voice in the movement came from a former slave, **Frederick Douglass**, who published his anti-slavery newspaper, *The North Star*. Perhaps the biggest attack on slavery would come from an unlikely place—a woman living in Connecticut.

> **TIP:** *Peculiar institution* was a term used to describe the southern system of slavery.

Harriet Beecher Stowe wrote a fictional account of an African American slave that would eventually become the second-best-selling book of the century, just behind the Bible. The book, *Uncle Tom's Cabin*, created an even deeper divide between North and South and became a major factor in the rise of the abolitionist movement. The book appalled southerners, who saw it as highly inaccurate and using falsities to further the abolitionist cause.

Finally, an economic attack on the institution of slavery would be seen in **Hinton Rowan Helper's** book, *The Impending Crisis of the South*. This was a different approach towards fighting slavery, and used the economy and industrialization as reasons why slavery was hurting the South.

Slaves looking to escape bondage would find allies in members of the **Underground Railroad**, a network of safe houses and secret passages that helped them find their way to the North or even Canada. This was extremely dangerous, and many abolitionists as well as slaves endangered their lives by participating. However, the work of people like **Harriet Tubman**, among others, was vital to securing freedom for many slaves.

Overall, the abolitionist movement took many forms, as there was no "right" way to defeat slavery. Back to Africa movements, political parties, and violence were all attempts to end the southern practice, but initially had little to no success. The thirst for more land consumed slave owners, who looked for more ways to profit from cotton, and the United States government was happy to oblige as **Manifest Destiny** dominated the country's agenda for the foreseeable future.

Westward Expansion of Free and Slave Territory

In 1820, the country was faced with a dilemma when the Missouri territory applied for statehood. The United States was at a perfect balance of free and slave states; Missouri entering would offset that balance and shift political power to the South. **Henry Clay** engineered the **Missouri Compromise**, a compromise between the regions that allowed Missouri to enter as a slave state, Maine as a free state, and, most importantly, created a system for the future by making the 36°30' N line a dividing mark. Any state entering the Union *above* the line would be free (except for Missouri) and any *below* a slave state. This important compromise helped keep the country together for over thirty years and many politicians saw it as sacred. All that would eventually change, as cotton became even more vital to the southern economy.

> **ALERT:** The Missouri Compromise was held sacred by many (including Abraham Lincoln) as the only thing keeping the Union together.

The Mexican War

The ideas of Manifest Destiny and western fever had taken over much of America by mid-century, with **James K. Polk's** election in 1844 a prime example of its popularity. When the dark horse candidate was elected on a platform of expansion, thanks primarily to voters from the south and west, America pressed firmly forward on fulfilling its Manifest Destiny.

> **TIP:** Manifest Destiny was a term coined by John O'Sullivan, which stated that it was America's mission, or destiny, to expand from the Atlantic Ocean to the Pacific Ocean.

After a brief spat with Great Britain over Oregon, Polk turned his attention to California. First, Polk attempted to buy the land from the Mexican government while also negotiating the Texas border, but was turned away. In response, he sent **General Zachary Taylor** and his army to the Rio Grande border. Tensions were high and fighting broke out, leaving 11 Americans dead. This event led Polk to declare war on Mexico, with a large majority in Congress approving the measure (although there were doubters, such as **Whig party** members, which included a young Abraham Lincoln, who declared that the decision to go to war was based on "spot resolutions").

It was a relatively short war, but its effects had great consequences in the United States, specifically regarding slavery. **David Wilmot**, a Pennsylvania Congressmen, proposed that all territories acquired as part of the **Treaty of Guadalupe Hidalgo** (1848) not permit slavery. The measure was defeated in the Senate, and what to do with the territory would be settled by the **Compromise of 1850**. Once again, Henry Clay came to the rescue, as the line created by the Missouri Compromise would cut directly through California, which wished to remain free. Clay's proposal included the following:

- admit California as a free state (adding to the North's political power)
- allow slavery to be decided by popular sovereignty in both Utah and New Mexico
- settle the Texas border dispute by paying the Mexican government $10 million

- ban the slave trade in the District of Columbia
- adopt and enforce a new, stricter Fugitive Slave Law (which was rarely enforced in the north, upsetting southerners)

> **ALERT:** The *Wilmot Proviso* reinforced the idea that slavery was a dividing and controversial issue. The failure of the act proved that the South was unwilling to relent on the practice.

The Kansas-Nebraska Act

In 1854, the Kansas and Nebraska territories were ready to apply for statehood and both saw the economic benefits of being open to slavery. **Senator Stephen A. Douglas** also looked to benefit from the territories when he proposed the **Kansas-Nebraska Act** to Congress. Douglas, who had presidential aspirations, needed southern approval to build a railroad through the central United States. To win over southern votes, he proposed that **popular sovereignty** be used to decide the slavery question in both territories. By effectively removing the line created by the Missouri Compromise, slavery could now spread into northern territories. When the bill passed, political outrage and citizen violence broke out in the territories—and even inside the walls of Congress.

People on both sides of the argument, pro-slavery and anti-slavery, flocked into the territories, hoping to swing the vote to their sides. Fighting broke out between them, leading to bloodshed and violence (termed **Bleeding Kansas**). The conflict grew so large that rifles, known as **Beecher's bibles** (after *Uncle Tom's Cabin* author Harriet Beecher Stowe), were even shipped with books to supply the anti-slavery forces in the fight.

This violence would last almost two years, and even make its way into Congress as **Preston Brooks** caned **Massachusetts Senator Charles Sumner** on the Senate floor in an act that defended the institution of slavery. In reaction to the situation created by the Kansas-Nebraska Act, a partnership of different, smaller political parties joined together to form the **Republican Party**. With the goal of stopping the spread of slavery across the country, Republicans would grow stronger as more people began to oppose the peculiar institution. However, this strength was found almost exclusively in the North.

ALERT: The Kansas-Nebraska Act is a key catalyst in the onset of the Civil War. It made the Missouri Compromise mute, it created the Republican Party, it caused massive violence, and it would be cause for such events as the *Lincoln-Douglas debates*.

The Dred Scott Decision

The final blow to the Missouri Compromise would come in 1857 via a Supreme Court decision made by **Chief Justice Roger Taney**. The case involved a slave, **Dred Scott**, who had been moved to the free territory of Wisconsin before returning to Missouri two years later. Scott argued that this made him free and sued, resulting in a Supreme Court case. Chief Justice Taney ruled against Scott, citing the Fifth Amendment of the Constitution (Taney claimed slaves were property, not citizens). The decision effectively ruled the Missouri Compromise unconstitutional and made all parts of the country open to slavery. This only heightened tensions between regions, and southerners were excited to end the question forever as well as open new territories to the institution. The decision would be hotly discussed and disputed, including during the Lincoln-Douglas debates for the Illinois Senate seat in 1858 (won by **Stephen A. Douglas**).

John Brown's Raid on Harper's Ferry

John Brown had been no stranger to violence in his abolitionist mission, as he took part in the fighting of Bleeding Kansas. After the Dred Scott decision, Brown attempted to arm slaves in Virginia in his greatest example of radical abolitionism. Federal troops ended his attempt after only two days, and Brown was hung for treason. The country was firmly divided over this event. Southerners pointed to Brown's radical activities as proof the North would do anything, including use violence, to end slavery. Northern abolitionists saw John Brown as a martyr for their cause, even as many others in the region spoke out against his use of violence. The events of the 1850s only further cemented what many in the country had feared: war would be the only answer to the question of slavery.

TIP: *Popular sovereignty* permitted the citizens of a territory to vote whether to allow slavery or not.

1860

In 1860, the country saw four candidates running for the White House, with three drawing votes from each other's bases. Northern Democrats hoped to run **Stephen A. Douglas**, but he wasn't popular in the South, leading to **John C. Breckinridge** being nominated as well. The Constitutional Party's **John Bell** and the Republican candidate, **Abraham Lincoln**, challenged both Democratic Party nominees.

The results of the election mirrored the events of the country to that point; the North voted for Lincoln and he carried every free state. Breckinridge and Bell held the South, and Douglas received 12 electoral votes, meaning that due to the population advantage in the North, Abraham Lincoln was elected the 16th president without obtaining a single southern vote.

> **TIP:** Thomas Jefferson and James Madison wrote the Virginia and Kentucky Resolutions in response to the Alien and Sedition Acts of 1798. They stated states had the right to declare federal law unconstitutional.

This confirmed what the South had long feared—no matter what they did they were still at a political disadvantage and their voices would go unheard. A last-ditch effort was made to calm the fears of southern slave owners by **Senator John Crittenden**, but to no avail (the **Crittenden Compromise** sought to restore the Missouri Compromise line). Following Lincoln's election, South Carolina voted to secede from the Union with seven states leaving before he had even taken office. Citing the **Virginia and Kentucky Resolutions** as support for their decision to protect states' rights, the president-elect addressed preserving the Union during his first inaugural address:

> *"I am loath to close. We are not enemies, but friends. We must not be enemies. Though passion may have strained it must not break our bonds of affection. The mystic chords of memory, stretching from every battlefield and patriot grave to every living heart and hearthstone all over this broad land, will yet swell the chorus of the Union, when again touched, as surely they will be, by the better angels of our nature."*

1861

After the election of Abraham Lincoln, with no electoral votes coming from the South, the president faced a crossroads in dealing with the **secession** of South Carolina and other southern states. As the Confederate States of America created their own constitution (one similar to the United States' but with provisions on tariffs and slavery) under President Jefferson Davis, Union President Lincoln faced a tough decision in regards to a federal fort in Charleston, South Carolina. **Fort Sumter** was in desperate need of supplies but had been blocked by southern forces. Lincoln had to decide: would he send reinforcements and risk starting a conflict or would he let the troops suffer? The president formally announced he would send supplies and provisions to the fort, placing the burden of what to do next onto South Carolina. The response was thundering, literally, as South Carolina fired its guns on the fort. The Civil War had begun.

> **TIP:** After the events at Fort Sumter, four more states joined the Confederacy including the state of Virginia. Richmond would become the capital of the Confederate States of America.

The Start of War

The original enlistment for Union troops was only 90 days, as Lincoln was optimistic that his army would easily defeat their Confederate brothers. The Union Army had many advantages, including a much larger population and a strong navy that dominated the waters during the war. Economically, the Union had control of the banking centers, factories, and railroads, and their provisions and weapons were never in danger of being in short supply. Perhaps the greatest strength for the Union would be their president; Abraham Lincoln would display his leadership skills throughout the war. Although there were struggles with his leadership style, including his tireless control of every decision (as evidenced by his shuffling of generals), Lincoln showed great vision and strength. His ability to retain the border states through martial law (and later the **Emancipation Proclamation**) was not without criticism, but overall he was seen as a strong and legitimate president.

Jefferson Davis, on the other hand, seemed ill-equipped for the position of president. Perhaps his biggest challenge had nothing to do with him, but rather the position of the Confederate states. Secession had been based on the idea of states' rights, so any attempt to create a stronger central government in the South during the war was met with resistance. Davis had little to give in terms of military leadership and the Confederate states lacked supplies, money, and a navy; instead, they placed much of their hope on using cotton exports to bring foreign support to their side. What turned out to be the greatest advantages for the Confederate states, however, were their dedication to the cause and their generals. The South had a cause they were fighting for, and they had the best-trained generals leading the charge on their own land. Many of the generals leading the South, including **Robert E. Lee**, had graduated from West Point and fought in the Mexican-American War. This experience, coupled with the ability to fight a defensive war on home soil, gave the South hope that they could hold out long enough for the Union to tire of the war.

Comparison of Union and Confederacy, 1860–1864

	Year	Union	Confederacy
Population	1860	22,100,000	9,100,000
	1864	28,800,000	3,000,000
Free	1860	21,700,000	5,600,000
Slave	1860	400,000	3,500,000
	1864	negligible	1,900,000
Soldiers	1860–1864	2,100,000	1,064,000
Railroad miles	1860	21,800	8,000
	1864	29, 100	negligible
Manufacturers	1860	90%	10%
	1864	98%	negligible
Arms production	1860	97%	3%
	1864	98%	negligible
Cotton bales	1860	negligible	4,500,000
	1864	300,000	negligible
Exports	1860	30%	70%
	1864	98%	negligible

First Manassas (Bull Run)

Most believed the war would be a quick exercise in northern dominance, including many in the South. The first major battle of the war was fought in Virginia near **Bull Run Creek** at **Manassas Junction**. Here, it was the leadership of a Confederate general, **Thomas "Stonewall" Jackson**, that made the difference. This battle all but ended the chances for a swift Union victory and a loud boom from the Confederate drum was sounded. The South had proven their abilities not only to the Union, but also to itself. Confidence was high in the South following the battle, as the rebel yell of the Confederacy was born. Lincoln's call for 1 million new volunteers after the battle was a wake-up call to those in the North who had been overconfident the war would end quickly. It would also lead to a major reorganization of the army, which included dividing troops between the Eastern and Western theaters, removing several generals, and Lincoln taking even greater control of military operations.

1862

Southern Strategy

By the start of 1862, the Confederacy was in a better position than the Union as their morale was high, they had been victorious in various battles in Virginia, and they were succeeding in continuing a war that no one in the North really wanted to fight. The original southern strategy was simply to wait the North out until they tired of war and simply let the Confederacy leave the Union. The Confederate Army did not actually have to win the war, only protect their land—it was the North that was fighting to save the Union.

President Jefferson Davis himself believed the best strategy for the Confederacy was simply to "survive." However, as victories mounted, General Lee led his army into enemy territory hoping to gain an even greater advantage: support from Great Britain and more importantly, their navy. Most of the South's cotton exports had been purchased by Britain and the Confederacy thought they could leverage those exports into foreign aid. But a victory in enemy territory would most assuredly prove to Europe that the Confederacy was a legitimate threat to defeat the Union, weakening it in the process.

Major Battles

Unfortunately for the Confederacy, the victory they so desperately needed did not come and the consequences would forever end their chances of gaining foreign support. The battle at **Antietam** would not only go down as the single bloodiest day of the war, with over 22,000 soldiers injured or killed, but the Union "victory" (which actually was a military draw) would keep foreign powers from supporting and supplying the Confederacy.

Great Britain had found a new source of importing cotton (from India and Egypt), and they were more concerned with President Lincoln's newly announced **Emancipation Proclamation**, which put the focus of the war squarely on slavery. The Union did, however, miss a great opportunity to pursue the retreating General Lee into the Shenandoah Valley, prompting the president to make a change in Union command.

Following the battle at Antietam, Lincoln would replace **George B. McClellan** as general of the Union in the east with **Ambrose Burnside**, primarily because he believed McClellan was too cautious. Burnside, however, would never be labeled as cautious and immediately led a disastrous attack on the Confederacy at **Fredericksburg**. The Union suffered heavy casualties, and the event highlighted the fact that the war had no end in sight. The Confederacy continued to push deep into Union territory, as the **Peninsular Campaign** under Union General McClellan proved unsuccessful. Confederate General "Stonewall" Jackson secured much of Tennessee, and by the end of 1862 the Confederacy was closer to the Union capital than their own capital of Richmond.

Perhaps the only bright spot for the Union in the Eastern theater would be at sea, as their superior navy was able to provide an effective blockade on southern ports. The Union successfully countered a Confederate **ironclad**, the *Merrimac*, with their own ironclad, the *Monitor*, in a battle that was the first of its kind. Prior to the *Merrimac*, ships had been constructed of wood for speed, but after this battle naval engagement would never be the same, as ironclads easily tore through their wooden counterparts. The Union blockade would remain intact and the Confederacy would continue to struggle to obtain supplies from their ports.

TIP: An ironclad was a ship made of and protected by iron instead of wood.

The Union had better success in their western campaigns under General Ulysses S. Grant. Their goal was to gain control of the Mississippi River and the port at New Orleans as part of their **Anaconda Plan**. U.S. Navy ships under **David G. Farragut** were able to take the port, while Grant's men led a charge towards Tennessee at both **Chattanooga** and **Shiloh**. These battles were bloody, terrible, and ended in victories for the Union that would upset Confederate holdings. However, both battles proved to the armies that the war would continue to drag on—with growing casualties.

> **TIP:** The Anaconda Plan was the Union strategy for victory in the Civil War that attempted to blockade the southern ports, to cut off supplies to the Confederacy.

Emancipation Proclamation

In 1862, President Lincoln realized the war could no longer continue simply as one to "save the Union." Northerners began to tire of the war and volunteers were down, but more importantly morale in the field was waning. He was also receiving pressure from more radical members of his party to take a stance on slavery.

Lincoln was weary of losing the important border states, where slavery was still in practice, so he had resisted calls for emancipation. With the military draw at Antietam, Lincoln saw his chance to change the course of the war and give the Union a greater purpose for fighting. On January 1, 1863 President Lincoln officially issued the Emancipation Proclamation, which freed all enslaved people in the rebellious states.

While the declaration had no legal effect on the war (Confederate states ignored the proclamation as Lincoln was not their commander-in-chief), the morale of the Union was immediately improved and the border states were able to keep their slaves. Soldiers now had a moral purpose for fighting the war, and freed slaves were now permitted to fight for the Union. The proclamation also kept Great Britain's government (which had already banned slavery) from officially recognizing the Confederacy due to pressure from its citizens.

> **TIP:** The Emancipation Proclamation was issued in September of 1862 and ordered that all enslaved people in the rebellious states would be free. It is important to remember that Lincoln was *not* president of the Confederate, or rebellious, states; thus, his words did not free any slaves.

1863

The turning point in the war would come in 1863, when Confederate confidence and morale came crashing down. Heavy casualties, the influx of new African American soldiers to the North, and difficulty providing provisions for their soldiers would finally catch up with the Confederacy. 1863 was not only a turning point for the war, but also for the society that took part in it.

War and Society

Following the Emancipation Proclamation given by President Lincoln in January of 1863, almost 200,000 African Americans came to serve in the Union Army. **Freedmen**, as they were known, had escaped the perils of slavery and the South to come and fight for the Union in an attempt to right the social wrongs of the peculiar institution. These added soldiers helped the Union gain an even greater advantage on the battlefield.

However, after joining the northern cause they still faced discrimination, as there was still racism present above the Mason-Dixon line. African American soldiers were segregated into all-black units, had only white commanders, and initially earned less pay for their service. They would find more support in western campaigns under General Grant (something that would not be forgotten during his election for president in 1868), but in general they saw less action than white units.

The most famous example were the 1,000 men of the Massachusetts 54th, who fought most famously in the **Battle of Fort Wagner** under **General Robert Gould Shaw**. They helped to rescue white troops and proved their bravery as the **Army of Freedom**. Overall, over 37,000 soldiers died in battle, including some who signed up and fought for the Confederacy.

The decision to turn the Civil War into a campaign against slavery was not popular among everyone in the North, as proven by the **draft riots** that broke out in New York City during July of 1863. Some whites, primarily Irish Americans, were upset that the poor were being sent to die in a war for African Americans. African Americans, along with wealthy whites, were attacked during the riots, which led to property damage and the deaths of over 100 people. The violence proved that racism continued to exist even in the North and that not everyone was pleased with the course the war had taken.

TIP: During the Civil War a drafted soldier could pay a "substitute" $300 to take his place in the army.

Role of Women in the War

Women, too, had a place in the war as men needed support both on the battlefield and back home. In the south, women took over the family farms and continued to take care of the fields; the North saw women working in factories. The greatest impact women would have on the Civil War, however, would be found directly on the battlefield. Inspired by women like **Florence Nightingale**, whose work in England encouraged the likes of **Dorothea Dix** and **Clara Barton**, the medical profession in America was forever changed.

The **Sanitary Commission** was created in 1861 to provide medical care for troops, while other women helped wherever they could. Women took on the roles of military nurses, tending to injured soldiers on and off the battlefield. While medicine itself was not always effective (and in fact sometimes more deadly than the wounds created by war), the introduction of women as nurses was a bright spot for the profession ,even though they had very little medical training. Barton, specifically, took her experiences from the battlefield and began the **American Red Cross** after the war. The war, along with the rights given to African Americans after it ended, would also be a catalyst for the **Women's Rights Movement**.

Major Battles

1863 was also a turning point in the war because of the number of casualties that resulted from the numerous battles. No loss was more devastating to the Confederacy than that of "Stonewall" Jackson during the **Battle of Chancellorsville**, at the hands of his own troops no less. Union troops, under **General Hooker**, were forced to retreat (while losing over 14,000 soldiers), but not before taking the lives of over 10,000 Confederate soldiers. This battle would soon have another war-changing consequence, when General Lee decided to make a push towards Washington D.C.

Over 50,000 men died during the three-day clash at **Gettysburg** as Lee led his troops into Pennsylvania. The **Battle of Gettysburg** is perhaps the most famous Civil War battle, due to its bloodshed and President Lincoln's famous speech afterwards. The Confederacy had hoped a victory at Gettysburg would turn the war back in their favor while also forcing the Union to finally end the war. General Lee's army in northern Virginia, flanked by **James Longstreet** and **George Pickett**, made would what would be their greatest challenge to the Union Army in the Eastern theater. President Lincoln had decided that the Union would make its stand at Gettysburg and by the second day the **Army of the Potomac** would hold its ground. On the third day, Pickett led a fatal charge directly into Union lines, which devastated the Confederacy, both militarily and psychologically. Lee and his troops were pushed back as a result of the battle, and never regained the offensive or the confidence they had when the year began.

In the Western theater, General Grant of the Union Army was continuing his successful push to control the Mississippi at the **Battle of Vicksburg**. This would be the start of Grant's strategy of **attrition**, which would become the key to his victories moving forward. The Union general surrounded and starved the city for almost a year, resulting in full control of the Mississippi River for Lincoln's forces and the position of general-in-chief of all Union armies for Grant.

> **TIP:** *Attrition* means the act of gradually reducing the strength or effectiveness of someone or something through sustained attack or pressure.

1864

As another year of war passed, so too did the passion for fighting for some in the North. With an election coming and no end to the war (or the casualties) in sight, many looked to an alternative to lead the Union. Those in the Confederacy looked to the election with great attention and hope, as selection of a former Union general for United States president might be their best chance at having their own country.

Political Situation

It seemed that everything was stacking up against Abraham Lincoln in 1864, as the economy, the number of casualties, and political support were all moving in the wrong direction. The effects of emancipation had worn off and it was replaced with war fatigue on numerous fronts, which were not confined simply to the battlefield.

Economically, the war was having a huge financial cost, which forced Congress to pass the **Morrill Tariff** as well as the **first income tax** in an effort to raise needed funds. These attempts to raise money would not be enough however, and the Union resorted to printing paper money, known as **greenbacks**, to help the war effort. Because this legal tender could not be redeemed in gold, the North would see inflation hit incredible peaks (it would also lead to a rise in "shoddy millionaires" who became rich selling poorly made products to the Union Army), even with an established Treasury Department in place.

Workers did not see much in terms of wage increases but the North did see a large increase in manufacturing. There were also great benefits to the war that would not be seen until well after its conclusion, including the **Homestead Act**, **Morrill Land Grant Act**, and **Pacific Railway Act**. However, the North continued to struggle with the continuing war as the number of deaths grew to numbers never seen before, or again.

> **TIP:** The *Homestead Act* helped to settle the Great Plains; the *Morrill Land Grant Act* helped create land for colleges; the *Pacific Railway Act* authorized the transcontinental railroad.

Cities and families looked vastly different as so many men left to fight, and part of the toll would be expressed politically. Northern Democrats saw a split within their party based on ideas of war and peace as **Copperheads**, or **Peace Democrats**, started a greater push to end the war. While their primary motive focused on "King Lincoln" and his war on slavery, many were drawn to the idea of ending a war that caused so much death and destruction to society. Volunteerism declined and, as the draft riots proved, support for the war was waning. This division would be fully seen as the next presidential election began to take shape.

The Confederacy faced many disadvantages from the start, as their very existence clashed with vital elements of government survival. The Confederate government also struggled to find ways to pay for the war, as many of its citizens had little money (the wealth of most plantation owners was based on their farms, not actual currency), resulting in the need to print money. This inevitably led to inflation, and by 1863 life would only get worse when a food shortage hit the women working the southern farms.

The situation was worse for Confederate soldiers, as they had little rations, supplies, or even clothing, which left many to resort to picking up after the dead in battles. Perhaps the greatest harm to the Confederacy came from what was initially a perceived strength: their ports. The Union Navy was much stronger than that of the Confederacy, and their Anaconda Plan had been successful in controlling both the Mississippi and many important southern ports. The Union blockade had borne fruitful results, keeping Confederate supplies from reaching their men. The Confederacy had been left to support itself with no outside help or provisions, leaving their only realistic chance for a victory the northern election of 1864.

Presidential Election in the North

Lincoln ran for reelection in 1864 but made some noticeable changes that included a new party name and vice president. The Republican Party had established itself ten years earlier, disputing the Kansas-Nebraska Act and the expansion of slavery. But as the war continued on, and many in the North began to question why they continued to fight (and lose countless bodies), Lincoln needed to find a way to unite his party while growing his support base.

Republicans renamed their party the **Unionist party** and selected War Democrat **Andrew Johnson** as his vice president in an attempt to combat the growing strength of the Copper Democrats. Running against Lincoln was a familiar face, former General George B. McClellan, who had a strong platform of making peace and ending the war. Many in the North, including Lincoln himself, thought McClellan had a strong chance of winning and those in the Confederacy saw it as their last hope. However, it would be the events that led up to the election, specifically the campaign of **William T. Sherman**, that changed not only the election but the war itself.

The Rise of Modern Warfare

At the start of the Civil War, traditional military practices were still being used, as many of the generals had trained at West Point. Focusing on a limited war and battles, fighting with muskets, and attacking in close-order formations seemed the basic plan for war in 1861. However, as technology improved and the war dragged on, the war would transition into one of attrition in an attempt to kill as many men as possible.

TIP: Another major change in the Civil War was medicine, as many soldiers actually died from disease or infections sustained by poor treatment on the battlefield. Amputation and gangrene were common, as was contamination.

This was made easier with the advent of deadlier weapons such as the rifle (which was more accurate at close range, could be used to identify targets at longer ranges, and could inflict more damage). The rifle would end up being a key advantage for the Union, as the Confederacy could not match the production or speed in which they produced it in the North. Minié balls were also introduced, a cylindrical bullet with a hollow base that expanded when fired, inflicting more damage to soldiers and increasing casualties. Additionally, cannons were used in new defensive ways, to take down bullets and also to shoot down lines of attackers. With all of the new destruction created by technology, strategies had to adapt, and generals began changing how they approached battles.

War in the West

President Lincoln's greatest hope for being reelected in 1864 was a string of decisive victories, which supported the Union's decision to continue with the war. Those victories would come courtesy of William T. Sherman, Grant's replacement as general in charge of the west. Sherman had a different vision for the war and his 100,000 men who followed him on campaign across the Confederacy. Destroying and burning everything in his path, Sherman gave a new meaning to the term "total war." His scorched-earth approach not only destroyed the homes, farms, cities, and infrastructure of the South but its effects would be felt for years to come (Sherman even told his men to bend the rail lines so they could not be used to transport supplies to the Confederates, effectively stunting their ability to advance their economy).

Not only did Sherman's men destroy everything in their path, they also destroyed what morale the Confederacy had left. When Sherman took **Atlanta** in September of 1864, the Confederates evacuated the city, and watched the flames rise as they left. This victory, coupled with another naval success by **Admiral Farragut** at **Mobile Bay**, was more than enough to secure reelection for Lincoln. The writing was on the wall; the Union was closing in on victory.

TIP: The capture of Atlanta was followed by Sherman's March to the Sea, which included a conquest in Savannah before moving into South and North Carolina.

War in the East

By 1864, Grant had left his post in the west to take over the Union Army, marching directly towards Lee in the east. His first major test was at the **Battle of the Wilderness**—as was usual for Grant, casualties were high and the fight resulted in a draw. It was what Grant did next, however, that showed Lincoln had finally picked his head general correctly.

Grant followed the Confederate Army into Virginia before making, in his own words, his only regret, at **Cold Harbor**. As fires broke out, casualties rose even higher because his men could not escape the flames, and when it was all said and done over 13,000 Union soldiers were lost (compared to 2,500 Confederates). Although he was upset at the result, Grant did not waver and he continued deeper into Virginia, racking up more deaths and a new nickname—the butcher. Lee and the Army of northern Virginia had been effectively reduced by the constant total war efforts of Grant, and was pushed back to their capital at Richmond. The war was nearing its end.

> **TIP:** The Army of northern Virginia was the primary fighting unit of the Confederate Army in the east, under command of General Robert E. Lee.

1865

The final year of the war saw a swift and dramatic turn following the successes of Union Generals Grant and Sherman. The Confederacy had seen far-reaching losses on the battlefield, in production, and, most importantly, to its morale. Many within the South saw it as only a matter of time before the Union was restored under the newly reelected Abraham Lincoln. As the Thirteenth Amendment was passed by the Senate at the start of the year, the Confederacy also knew that slavery would be no more, leaving the Confederacy to pick up the pieces scattered by Sherman's march to the sea.

The Fall of the Confederacy

Sherman had successfully liberated prisoners at **Andersonville**, the infamous southern prison camp, in late 1864, and then captured the important **Port of Savannah** while escaped slaves joined his march. He resumed fighting in the new year by marching north through the Carolinas, continuing his campaign of total war. Burning everything in his path, Sherman did not let his men forget which state was the first to call for secession from the Union, and South Carolina was nothing but ashes by the time his army reached the North Carolina border. Sherman was sure to leave nothing untouched, including businesses, homes, and even the capital of Columbia. The destruction would remain in the minds of many following the war, leading to resentment and bitterness.

Fall of Richmond

While Sherman was heading up the east coast, Ulysses S. Grant had forced the Army of Northern Virginia into retreat. Losing control of **Petersburg** and its accompanying railroad, Lee and the Confederacy had essentially given their capital of Richmond to the Union. All of the Confederate leaders, including government officials and President Jefferson Davis, left the city and took their records and valuables. As the Union arrived, they were greeted not by soldiers but by angry southern white men who had gathered to burn the city in anger.

Before long, Lee would be forced to surrender in Virginia at **Appomattox Court House** within the Wilmer McLean home. His men had no supplies and were dangerously close to starvation, and as a sign of peace General Grant allowed them to return home (even allowing them to keep their horses and giving them rations). Although President Davis attempted to keep the war alive, it was painfully obvious to everyone else that this was the end of the Confederacy.

Costs of the War

The Civil War would go down as the deadliest war in American history, with over 800,000 casualties before the Union was restored. The South was a shell of its former self—their entire economic institution of slavery had been dismantled, its infrastructure was destroyed and burned to the ground, and its government was now at the mercy of Northern Republicans. The North had more people, more industry and technology (including rail access), and, most importantly, more power.

The costs of the war were great on both sides, but the cost of losing was even greater for the Confederacy. It would take over 20 years for the South's economy and infrastructure to recover from the war, and it took even longer for its population to recover. Their political structure would also face changes in light of the newly-found freedom and citizenship of African Americans (however, there would be very few southern Democrats elected to the oval office over the next century).

Casualties and Losses in the Civil War

North (Union)	South (Confederacy)
110,000+ killed in action/died of wounds	94,000+ killed in action/died of wounds
230,000+ accident/disease deaths	26,000–31,000 died in Union prisons
25,000–30,000 died in Confederate	290,000+ total dead
prisons	137,000+ wounded
365,000+ total dead	436,658 captured
282,000+ wounded	
181,193 captured	
Total: 828,000+ casualties	**Total: 864,000+ casualties**

50,000 free civilians dead

80,000+ slaves dead

Total: 785,000–1,000,000+ dead

While the country mourned its lost sons and brothers, President Lincoln began to piece together his plans for restoring the Union, known as **Reconstruction**. Lincoln had always believed the South could never *legally* leave the Union; thus, they never *actually* left in his mind. He was piecing together a way to heal the nation from the Confederate "rebellion" when **John Wilkes Booth**, a Confederate sympathizer and former actor, shot and killed the president at **Ford's Theater** on April 14, 1865. The assassination of Abraham Lincoln would change the course of Reconstruction, as a Democratic vice president from Tennessee was left to clash with Radical Republicans.

RECONSTRUCTION

The period following the Civil War saw a divided nation attempting to heal from the wounds of a devastating war, as well as the death of their president. The Union was whole in theory but far from it in practice, as both sides of the conflict faced rebuilding after a devastating war.

For the South, it would be more difficult; much of the fighting had taken place on their soil and, especially after Sherman's March, civilization would need to catch up to the industrial world of the North. Not only did the South need to recover physically, but politically as well, as Congress was dominated by Radical Republicans who wished to punish the South.

African Americans had also been given the right to vote and few would forget the Democrats' role in starting the conflict as Republicans were "waving the bloody shirt" before each election. As African Americans faced a new day following the **Reconstruction Amendments**, the South would eventually return to many of its prewar practices, if only under another name.

> **TIP:** *Waving the bloody shirt* was a political slogan used during Reconstruction, blaming Democrats for the Civil War and its bloodshed.

Presidential Reconstruction Plans

As early as 1863, before Lincoln was assassinated, he had begun to formulate a plan that would allow the South back into the Union. As stated previously, Lincoln did not believe the South had actually left the Union (he believed in **contract theory** over **compact theory**), and instead saw them in a state of "rebellion." The president knew it was important to return the Union to whole as quickly as possible and did not believe the people within a rebellious state should be punished for what their government officials had done (but he did believe strongly that those officials should not regain power).

> **TIP:** *Compact theory* was the belief that the states had formed a compact in creating the United States, and therefore could nullify their agreement. *Contract theory* was the belief that the people, not the states, formed the Union.

Lincoln's plan for Reconstruction was called the **Proclamation of Amnesty and Reconstruction**, or the **ten percent plan**, because when ten percent of a rebellious states' voter population took a loyalty oath their state government could be returned. Under this plan, most Confederates would be given a pardon by taking this oath and accepting the **Thirteenth Amendment** (acceptance would also have to be part of the state constitution).

Republicans in Congress contested this plan, and the **Wade-Davis Bill** was introduced the next year in an attempt to challenge the leniency of the president's proposal. The **Wade-Davis Bill** required 50 percent of the state population to take a loyal pledge and refused to allow any Confederate to vote on the bill, for fear power would return to previous leaders. Lincoln refused to sign the bill however, and when Congress was away the president used a **pocket veto** to stop the bill.

Everything would change after Lincoln's death, however, as former War Democrat Andrew Johnson attempted to implement his plans for Reconstruction. The Tennessean faced challenges from his cabinet and the Republican Party in Congress for his plan's leniency. Although similar to Lincoln's ten percent plan, President Johnson made use of a pardon that would eventually allow many of the planter aristocrats who ruled the South before the war back into power. The president's plan took away the right to vote and hold office from all former leaders and government officials of the Confederacy, as well as those with over $20,000 in taxable property. Because of Johnson's use of the pardon, by the end of his first year the South's political lineup looked eerily similar to pre-secession.

> **TIP:** A *pocket veto* is an indirect veto of a legislative bill by the president or a governor by retaining the bill unsigned until it is too late for it to be dealt with during a legislative session.

Congressional Reconstruction Plans

During the war, the North saw a large shift towards Republican power as the Democrats were blamed for slavery and the Civil War ("waving the bloody shirt"). With a larger population and an ability to work with the president to determine how to readmit the Confederate states, the Republican Party did everything it could to protect its political power.

A group within the Republican Party, including **Senator Charles Sumner** of Massachusetts and **Senator Thaddeus Stevens** of Pennsylvania, pushed to give African Americans more civil rights following the war. The goal was not only to help African Americans, especially in the South, but to strengthen the Republican base in the region as well. It was clear that few within the South supported the Republican platform, but the passage of the **Fifteenth Amendment** would increase the voting population to include African Americans, who would most assuredly vote Republican.

The *Radical Republicans*, as they were labeled, saw their opportunity to push a stronger civil rights agenda, while punishing the South, following Lincoln's assassination. Congressional leaders butted heads with Lincoln's successor, President Johnson, but had the ability to go around him on many issues.

ALERT: Radical Republicans benefited politically from allowing freedmen to vote while also removing democratic opponents.

The greatest achievement would be the passage of the Reconstruction Amendments, the **Thirteenth, Fourteenth, and Fifteenth Amendments**. These were the first steps in granting African Americans freedom, rights, and suffrage (while also being catalysts for a stronger Women's Rights Movement). These amendments were part of a Congressional plan that included a rejection of President Johnson's plan for Reconstruction.

- The Thirteenth Amendment ended slavery in the United States.
- The Fourteenth Amendment granted citizenship to African Americans by declaring that all persons born or naturalized in the United States were citizens.
- It also forced states to respect the rights of citizens and provide them with "equal protection" and "due process of the law."
- Finally, it disqualified former Confederate leaders from holding state or federal offices while renouncing the debt of their defeated governments.
- The Fifteenth Amendment granted suffrage to African American males by prohibiting any state from denying a citizen's right to vote "on account of race, color, or previous condition of servitude."

TIP: The terms *franchise* and *suffrage* refer to giving a person the right to vote.

Congress followed up their rejection of the president's plan with a tremendous victory in the 1866 elections. Johnson toured the country in an attempt to attack Republican candidates, in the hope that they would lose their seats in Congress. However, the "swing around the circle" tour backfired, and not only did more Republicans win, creating majorities in both the House and Senate, but the president was large relegated to a bystander role in governing. The Radical Republicans were able to override his numerous vetoes to create three **Reconstruction Acts** in 1867.

- The former Confederate South was divided into five military districts, each placed under control of the Union Army.
- Readmission to the Union would now require not only ratification of the Thirteenth Amendment, but also the Fourteenth Amendment.
- State constitutions had to place guarantees for all citizens to be franchised, regardless of race.

The military-focused Reconstruction placed an army general as governor of the region and attempted to secure the newly-minted rights of African

Americans—the South was placed under martial law, with troops remaining in the region, until each state reached Reconstruction requirements. During this time, Congress also passed the **Tenure of Office Act**, which prohibited the president from removing a federal official or military commander without Senate approval. This was an obvious attempt by Republicans to keep President Johnson, a Democrat, from removing key Radical Republicans from the cabinet he inherited from President Lincoln. A key member of that cabinet was **Secretary of War Edwin Stanton**, the man in charge of southern military governments.

Johnson was well aware of the true motivations behind the act, and he tested its merits by promptly firing Stanton. The House would bring impeachment articles against Johnson in 1868, and the trial ended with Johnson remaining president by one vote (it was obvious to all that the act and trial were politically charged and not constitutionally based). Johnson would remain powerless for the remainder of his term, and Union war hero Ulysses S. Grant would be nominated and then elected president in 1868. The Republican president would owe much of his victory to large support from the African American voting population.

The Southern Response

While all of the Reconstruction requirements were officially met, the harsh reality saw few actually being followed, as many in the South found ways to continue to push racism and segregation. **Black Codes**, **sharecropping**, and **Jim Crow laws** all crept into southern society while Congressional leaders turned their attention to the economy in the North.

Black Codes developed as states began to restrict the rights of freemen. These codes had devastating consequences on African Americans and seemed to place them into positions of economic disadvantage. Black codes included the following:

- African Americans were not allowed to testify against whites in court.
- African Americans could not rent or borrow money to buy land, leading many to having to resort to signing work contracts, known as **sharecropping**.

Sharecropping was a new form of slavery in many ways. Following the war, most African Americans in the South could not read or write and only knew one job: working with crops. Because they had no money, homes, or employment they looked to what they knew—a field that had recently lost almost all of its workforce. Sharecropping allowed a worker (black or white) to plant and farm on someone's land. In exchange for use of the land, the sharecropper would then repay the landowner in crops. Most of these workers also needed money for the crops, food, or homes so they would exchange even more of what they yielded to the landowners. As the system continued it began to replicate a key element of slavery: dependency.

Jim Crow laws were attempts by southern states to legally deny African Americans the right to vote (which was now guaranteed by the Fifteenth Amendment), while also segregating them (most often a violation of their Fourteenth Amendment rights). In southern states, laws were passed that became voting "qualifiers," such as the following:

- **Poll taxes:** Any citizen wishing to vote had to pay a poll tax, or fee. While this was effective in stopping many African American voters, it also denied many poor whites the ability to vote.
- **Literacy tests:** Any citizen wishing to vote had to pass a literacy test, which was designed to stop freemen from voting. Again, however, many poor and illiterate whites were also disenfranchised.
- **Grandfather clause:** This was the most effective way of disenfranchising African American voters, as only those whose grandfathers had been able to vote could also vote. While almost no African Americans could navigate this clause and keep the right to vote, many poor whites could.

Segregation

The Fourteenth Amendment required that all people born or naturalized in the United States were to be given due process as citizens. This meant that African Americans were to be given the same rights as whites, but in the south this ceased to be the case, especially after the landmark 1898 U.S. Supreme Court case *Plessy v. Ferguson*. The decision in this case ruled that citizens could be separated as long as they received equal services or amenities. This legalized the ability of the South to create two separate societies—one black and one white. There were separate schools, and later separate water fountains and dining areas. The biggest issue with this ruling (as was the case with much of Reconstruction) was the lack of enforcement. Once troops left the South there were few reasons for the ruling to be followed, leading African Americans to face greater challenges with less support and resources. The ruling would later be overturned in 1954, by Brown v. Board of Education of Topeka Kansas.

> **TIP:** The term "freemen" was used to describe former slaves who were now free in the Union.

As governments in the South essentially restored the old ways of the past while "legally" oppressing African Americans, there was another challenge they faced in obtaining their rights. Racism and anger following the Confederate loss had caused new terrorist societies to form.

One such group was the KKK, or **Ku Klux Klan**, composed mostly of lower class white males who attempted to use violence and fear tactics to keep African Americans from voting, among other things. These groups wore all white with hoods and used torches to light their way. The KKK used many different tactics to oppress African Americans, including lynching in public and hanging. The KKK not only disliked African Americans, they also hated anything they felt challenged white power or kept white males from taking their "proper" place in society (including women's rights, prohibition, and any non-Catholic religious denomination). The focus on African Americans was much more apparent, however, following the increase of federal rights during Reconstruction, as KKK members believed African Americans were threatening their job opportunities and livelihoods.

In an attempt to combat all the discrimination and disadvantages African Americans were facing, Congress created the **Freedmen's Bureau** (Bureau of Refugees, Freedmen, and Abandoned Lands). This agency included the first unemployment and welfare offices and was often the only place where African Americans could find assistance following the war.

The Freedmen's Bureau gave food, shelter, medical aid, and education to freedmen. As many had no formal schooling, this would become important toward helping them become literate while also providing a chance to escape the South for job opportunities elsewhere. Some African Americans tried to move north for factory jobs or west in hopes of taking advantage of the Homestead lands offered by the federal government. Overall, the majority was forced to stay in the South and work as sharecroppers, however, as the Bureau received little support (especially from President Johnson, who used his veto power against it) and ceased to exist after 1870.

Other attempts were made to politically assist African Americans, such as the **Civil Rights Act** of 1875, but there was little support or enforcement and politicians would begin to move their attention towards a different focus. There would be no new civil rights legislation introduced to Congress until the 1950s.

There were some notable political successes for African Americans, including two southern African Americans being elected to the Senate (**Blanche K. Bruce** and **Hiram Revels**) and a few being elected to the House of Representatives. However, the majority of Congressmen remained white and the combination of African Americans and Radical Republicans who moved from the North would cause much anger in the South. Nicknames were created for two such groups—scalawags and carpetbaggers.

A scalawag was the name given to southern Republicans, while northerners who came to the South, most likely looking to make a profit, were called carpetbaggers and deemed corrupt. These derogatory terms reinforced the divide in the South, which was not only based on race but also political gain.

The End of Reconstruction

When President Grant took office, his administration quickly made Reconstruction its focus (amidst a myriad of scandals). **Redeemers**, or southern conservatives, had gained control of the South's government and many in the North had grown tired of the Radical Republicans' mission in favor of a focus on the growing northern economy. Redeemers brought back many elements of the previous South, including a hatred for taxes, a stronger focus on states' rights, and, most devastating for Reconstruction, white supremacy.

Democrats retook control of southern states and by 1876 they created a battle for the office of president. **Samuel J. Tilden** of New York received a victory in the popular vote but missed winning the Electoral College by one single vote. The Republican Party nominated **Rutherford B. Hayes** of Ohio and, due to their majority in Congress, was awarded a series of disputed Electoral College votes that kept Tilden from winning. The resulting compromise gave the Republican Party the White House, but at the cost of ending Reconstruction as Hayes removed the remaining federal troops from the South (Hayes also agreed to build a southern transcontinental railroad).

As historians look back on Reconstruction they do so with a divided view. On one hand, the federal government not only reintegrated the South following the Civil War but also rebuilt its economy and infrastructure into a powerhouse that would be realized during the Gilded Age. Furthermore, African Americans were given rights in federal amendments that would not only define them as citizens and give them suffrage, but also served as inspirations for future generations, such as was seen in the Women's Rights Movement.

However, the record is murkier when discussing the ability of African Americans to obtain and use those rights as well as the deepening racial divide. Generations continued to see segregation, discrimination, and racial tension as emblematic of the failure of Reconstruction to address the real problems.

SUMMING IT UP

- **Industrialization** changed the North, replacing traditional cottage industries and creating new transportation methods such as canals and railroads, which would ultimately connect the north and the west. The growing markets and increasing urbanization led to the expansion and diversification of the economy, which would help support the Union during the Civil War.
- While the North was becoming more industrial, the South was growing its economy around plantations—particularly in the cotton industry. **King Cotton,** or the belief that cotton was the "king" of the southern economy, came to account for more than half of U.S. exports by the start of the Civil War.
- In the **antebellum period** (before the Civil War), the U.S. population had increased greatly through higher birth and immigration rates, as well as increased lifespans and better quality of life. The increased population also increased wages and the demand for labor.
- The North and the South began to differ in significant ways economically, with the North favoring high tariffs to protect American industries, and the South opposing the limits these tariffs placed on southern profits. This would become a contributing cause of the Civil War.
- Slavery also became a point of opposition for the North and South, as the North moved away from slavery and toward industrialization while the southern economy depended heavily on the agricultural labor provided by slaves.
- The **abolitionist**, or anti-slavery, movement arose from the Second Great Awakening and its emphasis on religion and democracy. Publications such as **Frederick Douglass's** antislavery newspaper, *The North Star*, and **Harriet Beecher Stowe's** book, *Uncle Tom's Cabin*, helped the movement gain momentum. At the same time, members of the **Underground Railroad** were working to help slaves escape their bondage and move to free regions in the North and Canada.

- In 1820, the **Missouri Compromise** allowed Missouri to enter the United States as a slave state and Maine as a free state, to help maintain the balance between free and slave states. It would also create a dividing line for future states: states above the line would be free states (except Missouri), and states below the line would be slave states.
- As part of the resolution to the **Mexican War**, the United States adopted the **Compromise of 1850**, which admitted California as a free state, allowed Utah and New Mexico to decide slavery by popular sovereignty (popular vote), settled the Texas border dispute by paying $10 million, banned the slave trade in the District of Columbia, and created a stronger **Fugitive Slave Law**. Later, the **Kansas-Nebraska Act** would allow Kansas and Nebraska to decide slavery via popular sovereignty, removing the dividing line set by earlier compromises. This would be a major contributing factor of the Civil War.
- In the election of 1860, Republican **Abraham Lincoln** defeated Democrats **Stephen A. Douglas** and **John C. Breckinridge**, and Constitutional Party member **John Bell**. Lincoln was elected without a single southern vote, further increasing tensions between the North and the South.
- The Civil War officially began with the **secession** of the southern states, led by South Carolina. The newly formed **Confederate States of America** created their own Constitution, set their capital as Richmond, Virginia, and elected **Jefferson Davis** as their president. The war got underway when Union President Lincoln attempted to send supplies to South Carolina's Fort Sumter, which was under a blockade by the southern military.
- **The Battle of First Manassas** (a.k.a. Bull Run) showed that the war would not be the quick northern victory that many expected, with Confederate generals like **Thomas "Stonewall" Jackson** showing military strength. Other significant battles in 1862 included **Antietam**, which was the single deadliest day of the war (22,000 soldiers injured or killed); **Fredericksburg**, during which the Union suffered heavy losses; and the battle between ironclad ships *Merrimac* and *Monitor*, which was the first battle of its kind and ensured that the Union's blockade of supplies to the South would remain intact.
- In January 1863, Lincoln issued the **Emancipation Proclamation** as a way to resolve pressure from the slavery debate and change the focus of the fighting. The proclamation freed all enslaved people in the southern states. While the proclamation was not legally recognized in the Confederate states and thus did not technically free any slaves at the time, it improved morale in the Union states, and allowed freed slaves to enlist in the Union Army. More than 200,000 of these freed slaves would eventually serve in the Union Army.
- The **Battle of Gettysburg** proved to be a turning point in the war, due to heavy losses that stopped the Confederate Army's momentum. More than

50,000 Union and Confederate soldiers died at Gettysburg, and after the battle General Robert E. Lee's army had lost their offensive edge.

- By 1864, support for the war was declining in the North as well, and the costs of the war had led to an economic crisis that required Congress to pass the **Morrill Tariff** and the **first U.S. income tax**.

- **General William T. Sherman's** successful capturing of Atlanta provided the support Lincoln needed to win reelection in 1864, and showed that the war was coming to an end for the Confederate Army. Additional losses in the east to **General Ulysses S. Grant's** Union Army essentially pushed General Lee's army in Northern Virginia back to their capital.

- The Confederate armies ultimately fell in 1865, forcing General Lee to surrender to Grant's Union forces at **Appomatox Court House**, Virginia.

- After the war, the southern economy was at a major disadvantage to the industrialized North, with slavery dismantled and many plantations destroyed. It would take more than 20 years for the southern economy to recover from the Civil War.

- Lincoln's **Reconstruction** plans were meant to restore the Union, and bring the South back into the fold politically. The course of the Reconstruction plans changed when Lincoln was assassinated by **John Wilkes Booth**, a Confederate sympathizer. New President Andrew Johnson implemented his own plans for Reconstruction, which included taking political and voting rights from the Confederacy's leaders, government officials, and financial backers. However, Johnson also implemented pardons that negated the consequences for many southern political figures.

- Congressional Reconstruction plans included an aggressive civil rights agenda from the Radical Republicans. The **Thirteenth, Fourteenth,** and **Fifteenth Amendments** to the Constitution gave freedom, rights, and suffrage to African Americans. Congress also created the **Reconstruction Acts** in 1867, which divided the South into military districts, required Confederate states to accept the Thirteenth and Fourteenth Amendments in order to be accepted back into the Union, and called for all citizens to have the right to vote.

- Reconstruction measures were not popular in the South, and many states implemented policies that continued racism and segregation. The **Black Codes** adopted by southern states restricted African Americans from testifying against white people in court, and prevented them from borrowing money for land, which led to **sharecropping** (planting on someone else's land in exchange for crops) and former slaves' continued dependence on wealthy landowners. Additionally, **Jim Crow laws** attempted to prevent African Americans from voting by instituting **poll taxes**, **literacy tests**, and the **Grandfather Clause** (in which one could only vote if his grandfather had been able to vote—an impossibility for anyone whose grandfather had been a slave). The divisions were deepened with segregation, which claimed to create "separate but equal" services and facilities for African Americans and white people.

- Although the Union was technically whole in this postwar period, the Reconstruction period failed to address the larger issues of the divide between the Union states and the former Confederate states.

Chapter 4

The Civil War and Reconstruction Post-Test

POST-TEST ANSWER SHEET

21. Ⓐ Ⓑ Ⓒ Ⓓ   37. Ⓐ Ⓑ Ⓒ Ⓓ   53. Ⓐ Ⓑ Ⓒ Ⓓ

22. Ⓐ Ⓑ Ⓒ Ⓓ   38. Ⓐ Ⓑ Ⓒ Ⓓ   54. Ⓐ Ⓑ Ⓒ Ⓓ

23. Ⓐ Ⓑ Ⓒ Ⓓ   39. Ⓐ Ⓑ Ⓒ Ⓓ   55. Ⓐ Ⓑ Ⓒ Ⓓ

24. Ⓐ Ⓑ Ⓒ Ⓓ   40. Ⓐ Ⓑ Ⓒ Ⓓ   56. Ⓐ Ⓑ Ⓒ Ⓓ

25. Ⓐ Ⓑ Ⓒ Ⓓ   41. Ⓐ Ⓑ Ⓒ Ⓓ   57. Ⓐ Ⓑ Ⓒ Ⓓ

26. Ⓐ Ⓑ Ⓒ Ⓓ   42. Ⓐ Ⓑ Ⓒ Ⓓ   58. Ⓐ Ⓑ Ⓒ Ⓓ

27. Ⓐ Ⓑ Ⓒ Ⓓ   43. Ⓐ Ⓑ Ⓒ Ⓓ   59. Ⓐ Ⓑ Ⓒ Ⓓ

28. Ⓐ Ⓑ Ⓒ Ⓓ   44. Ⓐ Ⓑ Ⓒ Ⓓ   60. Ⓐ Ⓑ Ⓒ Ⓓ

29. Ⓐ Ⓑ Ⓒ Ⓓ   45. Ⓐ Ⓑ Ⓒ Ⓓ   61. Ⓐ Ⓑ Ⓒ Ⓓ

30. Ⓐ Ⓑ Ⓒ Ⓓ   46. Ⓐ Ⓑ Ⓒ Ⓓ   62. Ⓐ Ⓑ Ⓒ Ⓓ

31. Ⓐ Ⓑ Ⓒ Ⓓ   47. Ⓐ Ⓑ Ⓒ Ⓓ   63. Ⓐ Ⓑ Ⓒ Ⓓ

32. Ⓐ Ⓑ Ⓒ Ⓓ   48. Ⓐ Ⓑ Ⓒ Ⓓ   64. Ⓐ Ⓑ Ⓒ Ⓓ

33. Ⓐ Ⓑ Ⓒ Ⓓ   49. Ⓐ Ⓑ Ⓒ Ⓓ   65. Ⓐ Ⓑ Ⓒ Ⓓ

34. Ⓐ Ⓑ Ⓒ Ⓓ   50. Ⓐ Ⓑ Ⓒ Ⓓ   66. Ⓐ Ⓑ Ⓒ Ⓓ

35. Ⓐ Ⓑ Ⓒ Ⓓ   51. Ⓐ Ⓑ Ⓒ Ⓓ   67. Ⓐ Ⓑ Ⓒ Ⓓ

36. Ⓐ Ⓑ Ⓒ Ⓓ   52. Ⓐ Ⓑ Ⓒ Ⓓ   68. Ⓐ Ⓑ Ⓒ Ⓓ

69. Ⓐ Ⓑ Ⓒ Ⓓ

70. Ⓐ Ⓑ Ⓒ Ⓓ

71. Ⓐ Ⓑ Ⓒ Ⓓ

72. Ⓐ Ⓑ Ⓒ Ⓓ

73. Ⓐ Ⓑ Ⓒ Ⓓ

74. Ⓐ Ⓑ Ⓒ Ⓓ

75. Ⓐ Ⓑ Ⓒ Ⓓ

76. Ⓐ Ⓑ Ⓒ Ⓓ

77. Ⓐ Ⓑ Ⓒ Ⓓ

78. Ⓐ Ⓑ Ⓒ Ⓓ

79. Ⓐ Ⓑ Ⓒ Ⓓ

80. Ⓐ Ⓑ Ⓒ Ⓓ

THE CIVIL WAR AND RECONSTRUCTION POST-TEST

Directions: Carefully read each of the following 60 questions. Choose the best answer to each question and fill in the corresponding circle on the answer sheet. The Answer Key and Explanations can be found following this post-test.

1. The Republican Party platform of the 1850s was centered around the belief that

   A. slavery should be banned in all territories and ended as a practice.

   B. slavery should be banned in new territories but remain where it was.

   C. slavery should be allowed in new territories but only with a vote of popular sovereignty.

   D. slavery should be allowed in all territories but slaves only counted as three-fifths in voting.

2. John Brown's raid on Harper's Ferry had which of the following effects?

   A. It frightened northern abolitionists, and they unilaterally rejected Brown's motives.

   B. It frightened southern whites because the use of violence was attributed as a northern attack on the institution of slavery.

   C. It united abolitionists in their cause and was a major turning point in how they attempted to affect change.

   D. It forced the North to condemn Brown's actions and attempt to reconcile with the South following the incident.

3. Which is true about southern society in the mid-19th century?

   A. The southern economy was extremely diverse.

   B. Rich plantation owners had little political influence or power.

   C. A majority of southerners did not own slaves or large amounts of land.

   D. Many African Americans held political offices or positions.

4. The Compromise of 1850 was extremely controversial because it declared a stricter what?

A. Separation of church and state
B. Fugitive Slave Law
C. Tariff
D. Homestead Act

5. The Wilmot Proviso was significant because it attempted to do which of the following?

A. Ban slavery in all territories in the United States.
B. Ban slavery in all territories acquired from the Mexican War.
C. Ban slavery in all territories above the Mason-Dixon line.
D. Ban slavery in all territories that didn't allow for popular sovereignty.

6. Which factor is the most likely reason for Lincoln's victory in 1860?

A. The Democratic Party votes were divided among multiple candidates.
B. Lincoln ran on a platform of allowing slavery to remain but not expand into new territories.
C. The southern cotton economy had begun to shrink and the region was beginning to industrialize.
D. Abolitionist messages were reaching far more people and it showed in the final vote.

7. Why did the northeast and midwest develop an economic partnership?

A. The expansion of the railroad linked the regions while allowing fast and cheap transportation.
B. The use of canals allowed for more trade along rivers such as

the Mississippi.

    C. The northeast's desire for grains coupled with the midwest's growing capabilities created a likely pair.

    D. The refusal of the South to produce anything other than cotton made the North look elsewhere for trade.

8. Harriet Beecher Stowe enflamed the abolitionist debate with what book?

    A. *The Liberator*

    B. *The Impending Crisis of the South*

    C. *Uncle Tom's Cabin*

    D. *The North Star*

9. The Dred Scott decision was important for which of the following reasons?

    A. It created the idea of popular sovereignty, which allowed citizens to vote on the progress of slavery in a territory.

    B. It allowed slavery to move into any territory, regardless of the Missouri Compromise.

    C. It freed all slaves in Confederate territory.

    D. It formally legalized South Carolina's nullification of federal law.

10. Mid-nineteenth century America would best be described how?

    A. Politically and religiously diverse

    B. Economically and socially sluggish

    C. Territorially and diplomatically stagnant

    D. Demonstrating racial and gender equality

11. Which of the following examples would be the best evidence of Abraham Lincoln's leadership style during the early years of the Civil War?

    A. Lincoln's proclamation of emancipation to increase morale for the Union

B. Lincoln's institution of the draft for more soldiers

C. Lincoln's decision to allow the border states to retain slaves

D. Lincoln's constant changing of generals and leaders because of ineffective results

12. Which document would those in South Carolina reference as evidence that their decision to secede was just and legal?

A. The Missouri Compromise

B. The Kansas-Nebraska Act

C. The Virginia and Kentucky Resolutions

D. The Dred Scott decision

13. How did the Union view the Civil War at its start?

A. The North saw the war as a battle over slavery.

B. The North saw the war as a battle to preserve the Union.

C. The North saw the war as unwinnable.

D. The North saw the war as legal and understandable.

14. Which of the following would be a military strength for the Confederacy over the Union?

A. Banking and capital

B. Military leaders

C. African American soldiers

D. Factories

15. Why was the First Battle of Bull Run (Manassas) so important?

A. It set the tone and proved the illusion of a short war to be false.

B. It allowed African American soldiers to fight in combat for the Union for the first time.

C. It allowed Abraham Lincoln to announce the end of slavery after the Union victory.

D. Four more southern states, including Virginia, seceded after the Confederate victory.

16. What was Lincoln's goal at Fort Sumter?

A. To give up the fort as an act of peace

B. To surrender the fort in an effort to prevent war

C. To send provisions of food to troops

D. To attack the Confederacy in hopes of a quick war

17. The Confederacy's economic strategy during the Civil War centered on the belief that

   A. the North needed the capital created by the sale of cotton.
   B. European demand for cotton would lead to foreign aid.
   C. the use of a blockade of shipping would undercut northern merchants.
   D. northern factories would go bankrupt without cotton for clothing production.

18. The battle of Antietam was significant for the Confederacy for what reason?

   A. The Union removed General McClellan, a Confederate and peace sympathizer.
   B. The battle failed to gain European aid and open recognition from foreign powers.
   C. A large number of slaves had escaped to the North prior to the battle.
   D. Lee's weakened army wasn't able to retreat, forcing excessive casualties.

19. The battle at Fredericksburg was devastating for the Union due to which General's reckless strategies?

   A. George McClellan
   B. Ambrose Burnside
   C. Ulysses Grant
   D. "Stonewall" Jackson

20. What boosted the Union morale in 1862?

   A. The decisive victory at Gettysburg
   B. The Emancipation Proclamation
   C. The capture of the Confederate capital at Richmond
   D. The promotion of Ulysses S. Grant to head of the Union Army

21. Northern soldiers were diverted from their attack on Richmond in 1862 for what reason?

   A. To address the gains of "Stonewall" Jackson in Tennessee that included capture of food and supplies
   B. To address the loss of the Union capital of Washington D.C. to General Lee
   C. To support the Union blockade of southern ports such as

Charleston

D. To hear the Emancipation Proclamation given by President Lincoln

22. The southern strategy would best be described as?

A. Strongly offensive and aggressive

B. Patient and defensive

C. The Anaconda Plan

D. Total war

23. The Emancipation Proclamation was careful not to upset which group?

A. Republicans

B. Democrats

C. Border states

D. Abolitionists

24. Where was the Confederate military most vulnerable in 1862?

A. In military leadership, where many generals were inexperienced or young

B. Within the morale of its people, where many southerners questioned the war

C. In the east, as their capital and major cities were under Union barrage

D. At sea, where the Union Navy won many important battles

25. The single bloodiest day of the war was fought in 1862 where?

A. Antietam

B. Bull Run

C. Vicksburg

D. Gettysburg

26. What was the Confederate Army under command of General Robert E. Lee known as?

A. Massachusetts 54th

B. Confederate Nation of Soldiers

C. Army of Northern Virginia

D. Richmond Rough Riders

27. Why was the battle of Vicksburg significant for the course of the war?

    A. The Confederacy secured control of the western front following their victory.

    B. The Union marched from Vicksburg to the sea, burning everything in its path.

    C. The Confederacy had taken the offensive only to lose its greatest casualties.

    D. The Union secured control of the Mississippi River.

28. Where were African Americans most welcomed for combat during the Civil War?

    A. In Confederate regiments fighting for the South

    B. In Union units with other white soldiers

    C. In western regiments under General Grant

    D. They were not welcomed

29. How did the toll of the war and the shift to a war over slavery impact the North in 1863?

    A. With victories mounting more volunteers joined the Union Army.

    B. Riots broke out over the draft, resulting in the death of many African Americans in New York.

    C. Economic hardship and failure to monetize led to cutbacks in Union supplies.

    D. Large rallies and support for Lincoln led him to run unopposed in 1864.

30. Which of the following statements is false about the casualties of the Civil War?

    A. New strategies of formations and military tactics led to many lives being taken.

    B. New military technology found in weapons was deadlier than war had ever seen.

    C. Poor medical techniques and infection led to higher death rates.

    D. A shift to a war of attrition meant more focus on wounding and killing the enemy.

31. Which of these women made notable contributions on the Civil War battlefield in the area of nursing?

    A. Elizabeth Cady Stanton

    B. Clara Barton

    C. Florence Nightingale

    D. Susan B. Anthony

32. What factor led most to the Confederate's casualty rates being higher than that of the Union's?

    A. The Confederate Army had more men, which meant more men to lose.

    B. The war was fought primarily in the South, which mean more southerners were exposed to war.

    C. The Union focused on utter destruction and a strategy of no retreat, as opposed to the patience and thoughtfulness of the Confederacy.

    D. Production of rifles was slower and the materials for rifles were more difficult to procure.

33. What was the most devastating result of the battle at Chancellorsville in 1863?

    A. The Union victory led to over 10,000 Confederate dead.

    B. The Union loss led Lincoln to replace General Hooker with General Meade.

    C. "Stonewall" Jackson was accidentally shot by his own troops and died.

    D. A Confederate plan to invade the North no longer made sense after the loss.

34. 1863 was the high point for which of the following?

    A. Union morale

    B. Confederate confidence

    C. Freedmen

    D. Women

35. What general was most famous for his "charge" at Gettysburg?

    A. Grant
    B. Lee
    C. Jackson
    D. Pickett

36. 1863 saw the greatest northern victories in what two cities?

    A. Chancellorsville and Shiloh
    B. Gettysburg and Vicksburg
    C. Antietam and Appomattox
    D. Manassas and Bull Run

37. How did women and African Americans alter the course of the war?

    A. They added more support on the battlefield for both sides.
    B. They allowed the war to become about equal rights instead of states' rights.
    C. They were able to fight for the Union, creating a distinct advantage in the number of troops.
    D. They began to vote, which allowed them to influence political decisions.

38. What was different about Grant's approach following the Battle of the Wilderness?

    A. He retreated to higher ground found in the northwest.
    B. He used new weapons such as the Minié ball.
    C. He used new tactical formations.
    D. He pursued Lee after the battle and into Virginia.

39. What 1864 battle was Grant's greatest regret?

    A. Battle of the Wilderness
    B. Cold Harbor
    C. West Point
    D. Fort Sumter

40. What became the Confederacy's greatest hope in 1864?

    A. Pursuing Grant into Washington D.C. and taking the Union capital

B. Protecting Richmond and awaiting European aid to arrive

C. McClellan winning the election over Lincoln

D. Draft riots in the North over emancipation

41. What general did Grant leave behind to secure the west in his absence in 1864?

A. Hooker

B. Burnside

C. Meade

D. Sherman

42. Which is false regarding how new technology, such as rifles, changed the course of the war?

A. Close order formations were now more fatal and had to be replaced.

B. Firepower was more accurate and deadly.

C. Generals began wearing privates' uniforms to be protected.

D. Rifles could be used to shoot down other bullets or cannon balls as a defensive tool.

43. Sherman's total war was significant for years even after the war. Why?

A. It destroyed the infrastructure and rail lines of the South.

B. There were more casualties in his wake than at any other period in the war.

C. The victories forced the South to surrender the Confederate capital of Virginia.

D. The United States has used the strategy in every other war they have fought.

44. What was the name of the southern prison camp liberated by the Union in 1864?

A. Andersonville

B. Cold Harbor

C. Charleston

D. Appomattox

45. What was the name of the Union strategy that isolated the South using blockades?

A. The Anaconda Plan
B. Scorched-earth
C. March to the Sea
D. Attrition

46. Which battle, led by Union Admiral David Farragut, helped to deprive the Confederacy of badly needed supplies in 1864?

A. New Orleans
B. Atlanta
C. Potomac
D. Mobile Bay

47. General Sherman's Carolina Campaign would best be described as what type of war?

A. War of attrition
B. Total war
C. Guerrilla warfare
D. Patient war

48. General Lee and the Confederacy met where to surrender to the Union?

A. Appomattox Court House
B. Richmond, Virginia
C. Ford's Theater
D. Gettysburg

49. Who was the man who killed Abraham Lincoln?

A. Robert E. Lee
B. George B. McClellan
C. John Wilkes Booth
D. George Pickett

50. How was the Confederate Army treated after its surrender to General Grant?

A. Harshly as soldiers were stripped of clothing, weapons, horses, and mules.

B. Humanely, as soldiers were given rations and allowed to keep their horses.

C. Indifferently, as Grant tended to his own troops and ignored the Confederates.

D. As traitors; any Confederate was immediately put on trial for treason.

51. Which amendment to the Constitution afforded citizenship to African Americans?

A. Thirteenth Amendment

B. Fourteenth Amendment

C. Fifteenth Amendment

D. Emancipation Proclamation

52. The southern governments of 1865 (under President Johnson) were

A. extremely different from the pre-war governments; African Americans were afforded many rights and ex-Confederates no longer held office.

B. moderately different from the pre-war governments; new constitutions gave African Americans many rights but ex-Confederate leaders were reelected.

C. similar to the pre-war governments; new state constitutions failed to address voting rights for African Americans and many ex-Confederates returned to Congress.

D. nonexistent compared to the pre-war governments; southern governments were stripped of all powers and not an official part of the Union.

53. The Reconstruction Acts of 1867 did which of the following?

A. Officially accepted the Confederate states back into the Union

B. Impeached President Johnson

C. Gave African Americans the right of citizenship and the right to vote

D. Placed the South into five districts under military occupation

54. What term was given to northerners who went to the South after the Civil War?

    A. Scalawags
    B. Carpetbaggers
    C. Freedmen
    D. Sharecroppers

55. What was the greatest success of the Freedmen's Bureau?

    A. Obtaining the right of citizenship for African Americans
    B. Protecting the right to vote for African Americans
    C. Supplying the opportunity for education for African Americans
    D. Creating a Civil Rights Act (1875) for African Americans

56. Which group would be known by the term "radicals" during Reconstruction due to their belief in obtaining full rights for former slaves in the South?

    A. Democrats
    B. Republicans
    C. Freedmen
    D. Abolitionists

57. The withdrawal of federal troops and subsequent "end" to Reconstruction was brought about by which of the following events?

    A. The assassination of Abraham Lincoln
    B. The impeachment of Andrew Johnson
    C. The creation of the Reconstruction Acts of 1867
    D. The election of Rutherford B. Hayes

58. The impeachment of President Johnson was focused on Johnson's attempt to do what?

    A. Allow the Confederate states back into the Union before ratifying the Thirteenth Amendment
    B. Allow Confederate leaders to return to Congress and positions of power in the South
    C. Remove Republican members of his cabinet without the approval of the Senate
    D. Remove Federal troops from military zones in the South after the election of 1876

59. How would one describe the Civil Rights Act of 1875?

    A. Poorly enforced and supported

    B. Revolutionary and inventive

    C. Positive and effective

    D. Wasteful and corrupt

60. How would one best describe the legacy of Reconstruction?

    A. Successful, as many African Americans obtained greater rights and opportunities

    B. Successful, as the South was seamlessly integrated into the Union and extended new opportunities to those oppressed prior to the Civil War

    C. A failure due to the lingering effects of racial discrimination, sharecropping, and the return of Confederate leaders to Congress

    D. A failure due to the lack of infrastructure improvements in the South and lack of suffrage amendments

ANSWER KEY AND EXPLANATIONS

1. B	13. B	25. A	37. A	49. C
2. B	14. B	26. C	38. D	50. B
3. C	15. A	27. D	39. B	51. B
4. B	16. C	28. C	40. C	52. C
5. B	17. B	29. B	41. D	53. D
6. A	18. B	30. A	42. D	54. B
7. A	19. B	31. B	43. A	55. C
8. C	20. B	32. D	44. A	56. B
9. B	21. A	33. C	45. A	57. D
10. A	22. B	34. B	46. D	58. C
11. D	23. C	35. D	47. B	59. A
12. C	24. D	36. B	48. A	60. C

1. **The correct answer is B.** The Republican Party was not in favor of slavery expanding but believed that by simply containing it, it would slowly end itself. Choice A is incorrect because the Republican Party understood that slavery needed to remain in some places and believed it would eventually die out. Choice C is incorrect because the Republican Party did not support the idea of popular sovereignty as it gave slavery the opportunity to expand. Choice D is incorrect because the Republican Party did not want slavery to expand into new territories.

2. **The correct answer is B.** John Brown's raid was used as a form of propaganda in the South and portrayed as an act every northerner wished to partake in. Southerners condemned the act and were afraid more were to come especially after Brown received martyrdom in some areas of the North. Choice A is incorrect because Brown was seen as a martyr in abolitionist areas of the North. Choice C is incorrect because many abolitionists were still against Brown's tactics and the use of violence. Choice D is incorrect because while there was a short "cooling" period between regions, the North did not reject Brown's actions outright.

3. **The correct answer is C.** The majority of people living in the South did not own slaves and had very little land, and many actually worked on the land for other, larger plantation owners. Choice A is incorrect because the economy was dependent on one crop, cotton. Choice B is incorrect because rich plantation owners dominated southern politics. Choice D is incorrect because few to no African Americans participated in southern politics prior to the Civil War.

4. **The correct answer is B.** The Fugitive Slave Law was added to the Compromise of 1850 in order to persuade southerners to accept the loss of California. However, many in the North refused to accept the law or enforce it. Choices A, C, and D are incorrect because they were not part of the Compromise of 1850.

5. **The correct answer is B.** David Wilmot proposed that all territory acquired as part of the Mexican War should be free territory only. The Wilmot Proviso did not pass and instead the Compromise of 1850 was passed. Choices A, C, and D are incorrect because they are not part of the proposal made by David Wilmot.

6. **The correct answer is A.** The Democratic Party had two candidates, including Stephen A. Douglas and John C. Breckinridge, and the Constitutional Union candidate was John Bell. With the southern Democratic votes going to Breckinridge and the Northern Democratic votes going to Douglas, Lincoln had a unified Northern Republican Party behind him. Choice B is incorrect because while it correctly identifies Lincoln's platform, the South did not vote for him thus it was not a reason for his victory. Choice C is incorrect because it is false; the southern economy was very strong in 1860. Choice D is incorrect because there were still numerous places in the South that refused to accept an abolitionist message.

7. **The correct answer is A.** The creation of the railroad connected the northeast to the midwest, allowing a partnership of trade to develop. Because it would become America's largest industry the railroad also replaced river routes as the primary form of transportation. Choice B is incorrect because canals were no longer used as much as they had been before and the northeast was not connected via the Mississippi River. Choice C is incorrect because while there was a partnership based on grain, it was not directly why the partnership developed. Those in the northeast still had access to some grains but the use of the railroads made trade with the midwest more practical. Choice D is incorrect because there was still plenty of trade between the regions due to cotton.

8. **The correct answer is C.** Stowe's work, *Uncle Tom's Cabin*, divided the nation as northerners took it to be a literal account of what slavery was like; southerners saw it as pure propaganda created by a northerner who had never seen slavery in the South. The book became more popular than any other book in the United States after the Bible. Choices A, B, and D are incorrect because they were not written by Stowe.

9. **The correct answer is B.** The Supreme Court under Roger Taney cited the Fifth Amendment to declare slaves property, not people, thus allowing them to travel anywhere their masters' desired while making the Missouri Compromise unconstitutional. Choices A, C, and D are incorrect because they were not included in the court ruling.

10. **The correct answer is A.** By 1850, more Americans had a say in politics and shared their different opinions on slavery. At the same time, there were more religious offerings as the Second Great Awakening created a democratic view on religion. Choice B is incorrect as the economy was indeed growing especially the market for cotton. Choice C is incorrect as America was territorially growing through Manifest Destiny. Choice D is incorrect as the country was still far from racial and gender equality.

11. **The correct answer is D.** The constant shifting of generals and leadership is best evidence for the struggles Lincoln faced as a leader. Until Sherman's March to the Sea there was no guarantee that Lincoln would serve a second term and many saw these early changes as poor leadership. Choices A, B, and C are incorrect because, although all are true actions of President Lincoln, they came later in his term and were not characteristic of his early leadership style.

12. **The correct answer is C.** The Virginia and Kentucky Resolutions, created during the Alien and Sedition Acts, were used twice by South Carolina (during the nullification crisis in the 1830s and again in the 1860s) as support for states being able to nullify federal law. Choices A, B, and D would not be cited as evidence for secession, as they are related specifically to slavery, not states rights. Choice A is incorrect because the Missouri Compromise created a line in which slavery was legal. Choice B is incorrect because the Kansas-Nebraska Act put slavery up to a vote via popular sovereignty. Choice D is incorrect because the decision allowed slavery to move anywhere in the United States.

13. **The correct answer is B.** The Union under Abraham Lincoln declared the war to be fought over saving the country, not slavery (Lincoln even admitted that if he could save the union without freeing any slaves, he would). The goal was to have the Confederacy reenter the Union first and then deal with slavery afterwards. Choice A is incorrect because the Union did not fight to end slavery early in the war (as proven by the border states retaining slavery after the Emancipation Proclamation). Choice C is incorrect because the Union believed the war would be won easily and quickly. Choice D is incorrect because Lincoln did believe the South had the legal right to secede and after the war his Reconstruction plan after the war supports this.

14. **The correct answer is B.** The Confederate generals were vastly superior to those in the Union, specifically Lee and Jackson. Many from the South had trained at West Point and had battle experience from the Mexican War. Choices A, C, and D are incorrect because they were Union advantages.

15. **The correct answer is A.** The Confederate victory showed northerners that the South would not go quietly and that the war would continue for a long time. Choice B is incorrect because African Americans did not fight for the Union in this battle. Choice C is incorrect because Lincoln made no such announcement after the military loss. Choice D is incorrect because all southern states had seceded prior to the battle.

16. **The correct answer is C.** Lincoln declared that he would not send weapons to the troops at Fort Sumter but he would not let them to starve. He placed the decision for war on the Confederates as he was only attempting to supply his troops with provisions. Choices A and B are incorrect because Lincoln refused to surrender the fort. Choice D is incorrect because Lincoln did not wish to attack but instead prevent any war by sending only food.

17. **The correct answer is B.** The Confederacy believed that European countries such as Great Britain would come to their aid in an effort to preserve the cotton trade. However, other countries such as India began selling cotton and the Confederacy no longer held a monopoly that could be used over Europe. Choices A and D are incorrect because the North had diversified its economy and was not dependent on cotton for use in its factories. Choice C is incorrect because the North attempted to blockade the South, not the other way around, as the Confederate Navy was extremely weak.

18. **The correct answer is B.** The Union victory (and subsequent decision to make the war about slavery) kept European powers from joining the fight. The recent banning of slavery in places such as Great Britain coupled with the Confederate loss was enough to keep foreign nations from entering into a conflict against the North. Choice A is incorrect because although McClellan was removed after the battle, McClellan was not a Confederate sympathizer and had yet to promote the idea of peace with the South. Choice C is incorrect because slaves escaping wasn't uncommon and was not a very significant factor in this particular battle. Choice D is incorrect because Lee was able to retreat.

19. **The correct answer is B.** Burnside had replaced the more cautious McClellan and led the army wildly into battle at Fredericksburg with a full frontal assault, causing casualties and another Union loss. Choices A and C are incorrect because they were Union generals, but not in command at Fredericksburg. Choice D is incorrect because Jackson was a Confederate general.

20. **The correct answer is B.** The Emancipation Proclamation changed the course of the war for the Union, giving soldiers a new reason to fight and increasing the number of volunteers due to the newly formed direction of the war: ending slavery. Choice A is incorrect because the Union did not have a decisive win at Gettysburg in 1862. Choice C is incorrect because Richmond was not captured in 1862. Choice D is incorrect because Grant had yet to be promoted.

21. **The correct answer is A.** The success of "Stonewall" Jackson in Tennessee forced the Union to redirect troops to the west in an effort to address the heavy losses of food and supplies. Choice B is incorrect because Lee did not capture Washington, D.C. Choice C is incorrect because the Union troops did not change course to help with the blockade. Choice D is incorrect because the address was not given publicly.

22. **The correct answer is B.** The Confederate Army was able to fight on their own turf and advance when necessary; they used a strategy that was patient and opportunistic while more defensive in nature. Choices A, C, and D are incorrect because they better describes the Union strategy.

23. **The correct answer is C.** The border states remained in the Union and were an integral part of its success, providing food. By only "freeing" slaves in the rebellious states, Lincoln was able to maintain those border states that still had a use for slavery. Choice A is incorrect because Lincoln was a member of the Republican Party and many asked for a harsher stance on slavery. Choice B is incorrect because many Democrats (who were found primarily in the South) were upset. Choice D is incorrect because abolitionists were happy with the first step and asked for a greater stance on slavery.

24. **The correct answer is D.** The Confederate Navy was weak and no match for the Union Navy; this was a main reason they had hoped for European aid. Choice A is incorrect because one of the strongest Confederate advantages was their leadership. Choice B is incorrect because many in the South believed more strongly in the war than their northern counterparts. Choice C is incorrect because in 1862 the Confederate Army was very strong in the east and they held their important cities.

25. **The correct answer is A.** The battle of Antietam saw more blood in a single day than any other battle in the Civil War, with over 20,000 men dead or wounded. While other battles would have higher totals, none would be from a single day of fighting. Choices B, C, and D are incorrect because they did not have as many dead or wounded in a single day of battle.

26. **The correct answer is C.** The troops under Robert E. Lee came directly from the center of the Confederacy in Virginia, fighting as the primary regiment of the South. Choice A is incorrect because this was the name of the all-African-American regiment of the Union. Choices B and D are incorrect because there were no regiments with these names.

27. **The correct answer is D.** The Union victory gave them control of the most important river in the country and an important strategic region of the war, securing the west for the Union. Choice A is incorrect because the Confederacy did not win nor did it control the West. Choice B is incorrect because the March to the Sea came later in the war. Choice C is incorrect because both statements are false.

28. **The correct answer is C.** General Grant supported the use of African American troops and encouraged the use in the west (this would later be a reason he was elected president). Choice A is incorrect because African Americans were not welcomed by the South in regiments until late in the war. Choice B is incorrect because African American soldiers were kept segregated from white soldiers. Choice D is incorrect because the Union did allow African Americans in the war in their own regiments.

29. **The correct answer is B.** The Emancipation Proclamation changed the Civil War to a battle over ending slavery. Coupled with the length and high number of casualties, many in the North became tired and upset with the course of the war. When President Lincoln instituted a draft that seemed to target lower-class citizens (substitutes could be bought by the rich), riots broke out near the New York draft offices over the issue. Choice A is incorrect because the need for a draft proved volunteers were not increasing. Choice C is incorrect because the Union had instituted a monetary system and stabilized its economic situation during this period of the war. Choice D is incorrect because Lincoln was not widely supported and faced a difficult election period.

30. **The correct answer is A.** Old strategies and tactics continued deep into the Civil War, with front formations leading to more deaths when facing the new, more deadly technology of the war. Choices B, C, and D are all true statements about the war.

31. **The correct answer is B.** Clara Barton, later known for her work with the American Red Cross, created a name for herself during the war by tending to soldiers on the battlefield. Choices A and D are incorrect because they fought for women's suffrage but had no role in the Civil War. Choice C is incorrect because, although she was an inspiration for many women during the war, Nightingale was from Europe and had no direct contribution during the war.

32. **The correct answer is D.** The Confederacy often had to resort to taking weapons off the dead because they lacked the production and materials to create enough supply for its troops. Choice A is incorrect because the Confederacy had fewer men than the Union. Choice B is incorrect because, although the war was indeed fought mostly in the South, there were still fewer Confederate soldiers than Union soldiers in the war. Choice C is incorrect because the Union did focus on these tactics, but often at the expense of its own soldiers not the Confederates.

33. **The correct answer is C.** Jackson's death, a week after being shot accidentally by his own troops, was devastating to the Confederates because he was one of the strongest, if not the strongest, generals they had after Lee. The Confederates never recovered from losing Jackson. Choice A is incorrect because although 10,000 died on the Confederate side, that was not as big of a blow as the death of Jackson (also, the Union did not win the battle). Choice B is incorrect because although Hooker was replaced by Meade, this move was did not have a large impact on the war or the Confederates. Choice D is incorrect because the Confederates would indeed begin plans to invade the North after their victory.

34. **The correct answer is B.** The Confederate Army was advancing through Pennsylvania and Union fear was growing at the start of 1863. The continual changing of generals by Lincoln coupled with victories by Lee's army put Washington D.C. in his crosshairs. Choice A is incorrect because Union morale was sinking until the victory at Gettysburg turned the tide. Choice C is incorrect because slavery still existed in the country and freedmen (freed slaves) were still facing segregation and discrimination. Choice D is incorrect because women had been involved in many battles throughout the war as nurses, but 1863 was not a significant change in their position.

35. **The correct answer is D.** Pickett's charge on the heart of the Union's lines at Gettysburg was not only unsuccessful but led half of his 14,000 troops to their deaths. Choices A, B, and C are incorrect because they did not lead a historically memorable charge at Gettysburg.

36. **The correct answer is B.** The Union victories at Gettysburg and Vicksburg turned the tide of the war, leading the Confederacy to retreat while losing more men and supplies. This would be considered the beginning of the end for the Confederate States. Choice A is incorrect because the Union was not victorious at Chancellorsville. Choice C is incorrect because Antietam was in 1862 and Appomattox was not a battle. Choice D is incorrect because they are the same battle, fought in 1862.

37. **The correct answer is A.** The inclusion of women as nurses and African Americans as soldiers changed the course of the war, creating more and better support for both sides. Choice B is incorrect because the war never became about equal rights for either group. Choice C is incorrect because the Union already had an advantage in population and number of troops so just their inclusion alone did not change the course of the war. Choice D is incorrect because neither group could vote during the war.

38. **The correct answer is D.** The Union and its generals had rarely followed the Confederates into southern territory after a retreat. In 1864, Grant continually pursued and pushed Lee back in an all-out furious attack that resulted in high casualties. Choice A is incorrect because there was no Union retreat. Choice B is incorrect because new weapons had been used throughout the war. Choice C is incorrect because new formations were rarely if ever used during the war, which led to more casualties because of the new technology.

39. **The correct answer is B.** The Battle at Cold Harbor saw Grant obtain a new nickname, the Butcher. With high casualties that resulted from a full-on assault that was coupled with fires his men could not retreat from, Grant believed this to be the only battle he regretted. Choice A is incorrect because it was a decisive victory for Grant. Choice C is incorrect because it is a military school, not a battle. Choice D is incorrect because Grant was not involved in the first shots of the Civil War at Fort Sumter.

40. **The correct answer is C.** By 1864, the only hope remaining for the Confederate States would be peace, and former Union General George McClellan ran on a platform of peace if he won. For a time it looked as though he would win, with many in the North tiring of the war and unhappy with its number of casualties. Choices A, B, and D are incorrect because all these events had passed and no longer seemed viable options for Confederate victory.

41. **The correct answer is D.** William T. Sherman was Grant's most trusted general and placed in charge of securing the West while he pursued Lee. Choices A, B, and C are incorrect because they were not left in command by Grant.

42. **The correct answer is D.** Cannons, not rifles, were used as defensive tools during the Civil War. While rifles became more accurate, they were still used as offensive tools. Choices A, B, and C are incorrect because they are all true of modern warfare during the Civil War.

43. **The correct answer is A.** The South was placed almost 20 years behind the North in terms of infrastructure and economy following the war, with a big reason being Sherman's scorched-earth tactics that destroyed the South and its railways (Sherman's men bent the lines behind them as they marched to the sea). Choice B is incorrect because other battles had more casualties; Sherman's greatest destruction came to the land and homes, not people. Choice C is incorrect because Sherman did not march to the Confederate capital. Choice D is incorrect because this strategy has not been used in every battle since.

44. **The correct answer is A.** Andersonville was a notorious southern prison camp that saw deplorable conditions and barely any rations for captured Union soldiers. Choices B, C, and D are incorrect because they were not prison camps.

45. **The correct answer is A.** The Anaconda Plan was a two-part process that included taking control of the Mississippi River and implementing a blockade on Confederate ports to cut off its supplies. By 1864, the plan had been successful and Confederate troops were in dire need of supplies. Choices B and C are incorrect because scorched-earth was how Sherman handled his march to the sea, burning everything in his wake. Choice D is incorrect because attrition was the constant wearing down of an opponent; while it was part of the Union strategy, it did not specifically isolate the South.

46. **The correct answer is D.** The Union Navy was sure to uphold the blockade on southern ships, stopping important shipments from arriving to reinforce the Confederates at Mobile Bay. Choices A, B, and C are incorrect because they were not naval battles that supported the blockade in 1864.

47. **The correct answer is B.** Sherman marched through Carolina with a goal to attack Lee's army and never let secession be an option again. He burned everything in sight with no regard for anything in his path. Choice A is incorrect because the march was not focused on wearing down the enemy, but destroying it. Choice C is incorrect because Sherman's march was not hidden and continued to destroy resources head-on with all of his troops. Choice D is incorrect because Sherman pushed through the region quickly without pause.

48. **The correct answer is A.** Generals Grant and Lee met at Appomattox in the McLean House where the Confederates officially surrendered to the Union. Choice B is incorrect because it is not as specific as choice A. Choice C and D are incorrect because General Lee did not surrender at these places.

49. **The correct answer is C.** The assassination of President Lincoln took place at Ford's Theater when John Wilkes Booth, former actor and Confederate sympathizer, shot him. Choices A, B, and D are incorrect because they were not the assassin.

50. **The correct answer is B.** Grant allowed for a respectful surrender that had a happy effect on the troops. Allowing the Confederates to keep their horses and mules would give them a chance to better plant their crops the following year. Choices A, C, and D are incorrect because they are false statements that didn't happen.

51. **The correct answer is B.** The Fourteenth Amendment states, "All persons born or naturalized in the United States and subject to the jurisdiction thereof, are citizens of the United States and of the State wherein they reside. No State shall make or enforce any law which shall abridge the privileges or immunities of citizens of the United States; nor shall any State deprive any person of life, liberty, or property, without due process of law; nor deny to any person within its jurisdiction the equal protection of the laws." Choice A is incorrect because this amendment ended slavery. Choice C is incorrect because this amendment gave African Americans the right to vote. Choice D is incorrect because it was not an amendment and only freed slaves in rebellious states during the war.

52. **The correct answer is C.** The South was easily able to return to the Union under President Johnson and many former Confederate leaders took back their positions of power in politics. States, while having to ratify the Thirteenth amendment, did not support or endorse African Americans voting in their constitutions (while doing nothing to curb Jim Crow laws). Choice A is incorrect because African Americans struggled to practice their rights under governments that included former Confederate leaders. Choice B is incorrect because new state constitutions did not support African American rights and did more to confine them than help. Choice D is incorrect because southern governments regained powers relatively quickly and rejoined the Union.

53. **The correct answer is D.** The act declared the governments recognized by Johnson inoperative while dividing them into five military districts, each with military supervision. Choices A, B, and C are incorrect because they were not part of the Reconstruction Act of 1867.

54. **The correct answer is B.** *Carpetbagger* was a derogatory term given to a person from the North who moved to the South attempting to make profit off the war-torn area. Choice A is incorrect because it was a term given to a southerner who supported the Republicans in the North. Choice C is incorrect because it was a term for freed slaves. Choice D is incorrect because it was a term for freed slaves or poor whites who worked on plantations after the war, using their labor as trade for wages and housing.

55. **The correct answer is C.** The Freedmen's Bureau was an agency created to help freed slaves, African Americans, and poor whites. It was most successful in creating a welfare-like system that gave African Americans a place to become educated, job skills, and even a place to stay. While it was underfunded by the federal government and ended relatively quickly, it still helped many freed slaves and African Americans learn to read and write. Choice A is incorrect because that right was obtained by the Thirteenth Amendment. Choice B is incorrect because the Freedmen's Bureau was not able to protect this right in the South as Jim Crow laws and violence often stopped African Americans from voting. Choice D is incorrect because the Freedmen's Bureau was not responsible for this act being created.

56. **The correct answer is B.** Republicans were known as "radicals" because of their stance on rights for African Americans. Choices A, C, and D are incorrect because they were not described by the term "radical" during Reconstruction.

57. **The correct answer is D.** The election of 1876 saw a compromise that gave Republicans control of the presidency (Rutherford B. Hayes) in exchange for removing troops from the South. Choices A, B, and C are incorrect because they were not the reason federal troops left the South.

58. **The correct answer is C.** Johnson, a War Democrat, had come into office after Lincoln's election and wanted to place members into his own cabinet. When he attempted to remove his war secretary, he was in violation of the Tenure of Office Act. Choice A is incorrect because all states ratified the amendment before reentering the Union. Choice B is incorrect because even though Johnson allowed this to happen it was not in violation of any law. Choice D is incorrect because Johnson was not in office during this period.

59. **The correct answer is A.** The Civil Rights Act of 1875 would be the last time until the 1950s the federal government attempted to procure the rights of African Americans. The act itself saw little enforcement in the South, from southern governments or the federal government. Choice B is incorrect because the act attempted to continue the rights created in the Thirteenth, Fourteenth, and Fifteenth Amendments and took no new steps to securing rights for African Americans. Choice C is incorrect because the act was just the opposite. Choice D is incorrect because there was no corruption with the act, only a lack of enforcement.

60. **The correct answer is C.** While some improvements were made in areas such as infrastructure and federal legislation, discrimination by Jim Crow laws and sharecropping remained in the South following the war. Many African Americans continued to struggle to gain equality and many white leaders from before the war returned to positions of power. Choice A is incorrect because while African Americans did gain more rights and even political office, the majority struggled to practice those rights in the South. Choice B is incorrect because there were many struggles with bringing the South back into the Union and equality was not found for many after it. Choice D is incorrect because there were some improvements to infrastructure and a voting amendment was indeed passed (Fifteenth Amendment) even though it was not often followed.

Printed in the USA
CPSIA information can be obtained
at www.ICGtesting.com
JSHW012043140824
68134JS00033B/3241